From Ancient Myth to Modern Healing

D0139848

This book is about the energy personified by the classical Greek goddess Themis, who brought her divine and natural 'right order' to gods and humans, and who still presides over law courts as the figure of Justice.

The ancient stories of the goddess weave through these chapters to illuminate how *themis* energy is at work today. The authors explore psychological healing in individuals and relate this to new research in neurocardiology on the subtle interactions of body and mind. They show how the international movement for restorative justice is drawing on the same healing tools to benefit victims and offenders alike. And they evoke the extraordinary story of the South African Truth and Reconciliation Commission, which shows the world how *themis* energy can help transform a ravaged society.

This book deepens understanding of the psychological urge towards healing and wholeness and offers exciting insights into Jung's approach to the relationship between individual and collective psychology. It will appeal to psychotherapists, to lawyers and others concerned with the failure of current criminal justice systems, and to people involved in religious, political and other groups that seek to build communities which can encompass and even celebrate diversity rather than rejecting it in fear.

Pamela Donleavy, J.D. is a Jungian Analyst in private practice in Arlington, MA. She is a former state and federal prosecutor in Philadelphia. Pamela is the past President of the New England Society of Jungian Analysts, is on the Board of Directors of the National Association for the Advancement of Psychoanalysis, and is on the faculty of the C. G. Jung Institute–Boston, and the Assisi Institute in Vermont. She lectures widely, and is the author of several articles in Jungian journals.

Ann Shearer is a Jungian Analyst in London and former Convenor of the Independent Group of Analytical Psychologists, for which she still teaches. She previously worked as a journalist and international consultant in social welfare. More recently, she was a Royal Literary Fund Writing Fellow at Imperial College, London. Her published articles have particularly focused on aspects of mythology and psychology, and her books include *Disability: Whose Handicap?* (1981), *Building Community* (1985), *Woman: Her Changing Image* (1987) and *Athene: Image and Energy* (1996).

From Ancient Myth to Modern Healing

THEMIS: Goddess of Heart–Soul, Justice and Reconciliation

Pamela Donleavy and Ann Shearer

Routledge
Taylor & Francis Group

LONDON AND NEW YORK

First published 2008
by Routledge
27 Church Road, Hove, East Sussex BN3 2FA

Simultaneously published in the USA and Canada
by Routledge
270 Madison Avenue, New York NY 10016

*Routledge is an imprint of the Taylor & Francis Group,
an Informa business*

Typeset in Times by
RefineCatch Limited, Bungay, Suffolk
Printed and bound in Great Britain by
TJ International Limited, Padstow, Cornwall
Paperback cover design by Gerald Myers

British Library Cataloguing in Publication Data
A catalogue record for this book is available from the British Library

Library of Congress Cataloging-in-Publication Data
Donleavy, Pamela, 1949–
    From ancient myth to modern healing : Themis, goddess of heart-
soul, justice and reconciliation / Pamela Donleavy and Ann Shearer.
        p. cm.
    Includes bibliographical references and index.
    ISBN 978–0–415–44804–8 (hardback) – ISBN 978–0–415–
44805–5 (pbk.) 1. Themis (Greek deity) 2. Restorative justice.
3. Spiritual healing. I. Shearer, Ann, 1943– II. Title.
    BL820.T47D66 2008
    150.19′54–dc22   2007050582

ISBN: 978–0–415–44804–8 (hbk)
ISBN: 978–0–415–44805–5 (pbk)

Contents

List of illustrations

Acknowledgements

The authors and publisher are grateful to the following for their permission to reproduce passages from copyright material and illustrations as follows:

Extracts from Jung, C. G.: *Collected Works of C. G. Jung.* © 1977 Princeton University Press. Reprinted by permission Princeton University Press and Jung, C. G.: *Collected Works of C. G. Jung* © 1977 Routledge. Reproduced by permission of Taylor & Francis Books Ltd. Permission of A P Watt Ltd on behalf of Gráinne Yeats for extract from the poem 'The Second Coming' in *Collected Poems*, ed. Augustine Martin, London, Vintage; poem by Billy Collins, 'Another Reason Why I Don't Keep a Gun in the House' from *The Apple That Astonished Paris*. Copyright © 1988, 1996 by Billy Collins. Used by permission of the University of Arkansas Press, *www.uapress.com*; extract from *No Future Without Forgiveness* by Desmond Tutu, 1999, Random House, Inc.; extract © 1994 Nelson Mandela. Reproduced from *Long Walk to Freedom* by Nelson Mandela by kind permission of Little, Brown Book Group; 'Diana' for permission to use seven drawings (Figures 2.1, 2.4, 3.1, 3.2, 3.4, 3.5, 3.6); ALINARI Archives, Florence (Figure 2.2); Herakleion Archaeological Museum, Crete, Hellenic Ministry of Culture – Archaeological Receipts Fund (Figure 3.4); Bildarchiv Preussischer Kulturbesitz/Art Resource, New York (Figures 3.7 and 5.3); Institute of HeartMath © Copyright Institute of HearthMath. Courtesy Institute of HeartMath Research Center (Figures 4.1, 4.2, 4.3, 4.4); Anna Goldmuntz (Figure 4.5); German Archaeological Institute, Photographer: kein Eintrag, DAI, DAI-Neg.-No. D-DAI-ATH-Delphi 133 (Figure 5.1); Delphi Archaeological Museum, Hellenic Ministry of Culture – Archaeological Receipts Fund (Figure 5.2); Photonews Service Ltd, London (Figure 6.1); Gabe Brammer and Bob Brammer, Iowa Attorney General's Office (Figure 6.2); *For Counsel Inc., the Catalog for Lawyers* (Figure 6.3); woodcut by Albrecht Durer, illustration from Sebastian Brant's 1509 book: *This present boke named the shyp of folys*, provided by the Beinecke Rare Book and Manuscript Library, Yale University Library (Figure 6.4); woodcut by Pieter Breugel, courtesy of Bibliothèque Royale de Belgique, Bruxelles, SII 135128.

Special thanks to Jules Cashford, for generous permission to quote from her translation of *The Homeric Hymn to Apollo* and to her and Richard Davis for help with sources.

Particular appreciation to 'Diana', 'John' and 'Jennifer', who have allowed their stories to be told. Their names and identifying information have been changed to protect their anonymity.

Pamela would like to dedicate this book to her husband, Paul Goldmuntz, whose humor, support, and love make life so special; and to her children of the heart: Anna and Ben Goldmuntz, Jason Eckenberger, and Patty McIntosh.

Prologue

Themis is a hidden goddess. She is not one of the twelve Olympians who sit on their golden thrones and carry the very definition of the gods of the Greeks. But in a sense she is below and above them all. Born a Titan, of an older race than they, she is often hailed as the incarnation of eternal, inexhaustible Earth herself, and she brings an ancient wisdom to their ordering of the world of gods and humans. Some say she is the first wife of Zeus, some the second, drawing on her prophetic powers as the original Delphic oracle to whisper her counsel in his ear. On Olympus, she brings together the goddesses and gods, and commands their feasts. On Earth, she draws together human beings, both individually and in social assembly. Her very name means an ancient, divine law, a right order established by nature itself for the living together of gods and humans.[1]

What relevance can this ancient deity and these stories have for the contemporary Western world? To modern understanding, grown up through centuries of opposition between spirit and matter, 'divine' and 'natural' can seem incompatible. Many people these days have little sense of what it would mean to live in harmony with 'the gods'. The idea of 'right order' can seem threatening, a bullying imposition of uniformity that takes no heed of individual difference. This is a very different world from the one in which Themis was originally venerated, where 'divine' and natural' were one and the same thing; to live in harmony with the gods was the most important aim; and the idea of 'right order' suggested a harmony that encompassed the whole diversity of the universe. Yet while Themis is hidden, she is also, paradoxically, one of the few ancient goddesses to be everywhere on show, in the West and beyond. Her image and the energy it carries have come through the generations as that of Justice herself: Themis is the often blindfolded figure with sword and scales who presides over law courts, as a reminder to those who administer human justice of the ancient underlying principle towards which they strive. So it seems that humans need the goddess still.

What might that mean? When the stories and images of Themis are seen as metaphoric precursors of today's psychological understandings, then they immediately become relevant. They point to a powerful and inherent psychological capacity to bring together and contain disparate energies in a work of healing or making more whole. In a world where the inner conflict of so many individuals echoes the terrible destruction of warring nations and sects, it seems important to try to understand more about this, and how it might be encouraged. That is what this book is about.

In a sense, the authors are both daughters of Themis. Pamela Donleavy was a state and federal prosecutor in Philadelphia where she investigated and prosecuted public corruption cases involving numerous judges, lawyers and public officials. During her last years as a prosecutor, she helped to create Urban Genesis, a non-profit organization affiliated with the District Attorney's Office, where she was able to help hundreds of individuals in the city's most devastated areas to stabilize and revitalize their neighbourhoods. Ann Shearer is the daughter of a distinguished High Court judge in Scotland, and grew up with a sense of 'justice' as a concept over and above human laws: she has a teenage memory of visiting her father's court and realizing with some awe that he could not smile at her, because in this place he represented something other than 'her father'. Ann worked as a social welfare journalist for many years, and was active in campaigns and projects that sought to bring long-denied human and civic rights to people with disabilities. Both of us are now Jungian analysts, and it is Jung's approach to psychology that informs this book.

For Jung, the images of those ancient gods and goddesses and the qualities that people attributed to them carried the archetypal energies that underlie all human experience, in our time as in theirs; they were projected images of powerful dynamics experienced by the human psyche. We can never know an archetype in itself – it lies too deep in the collective unconscious of humanity for that. If we approach its power too near, as the ancients knew when they trespassed on the terrains of their gods, we can lose that precious consciousness for which humankind has striven for so long, and forfeit our sight, our sanity, or both. But we can intimate the psychological power and potential of an archetype through the images it creates, the emotions these engender – and by spending time with the tales of the gods and goddesses which still contain and give expression to its otherwise overwhelming energy. The mythographer Joseph Campbell puts it poetically: 'Myth is the secret opening through which the inexhaustible energies of the cosmos pour into human cultural manifestation.'[2]

Western consciousness has grown very far from its mythic roots. For the ancients, seemingly random acts of destruction or good fortune might be attributed to Zeus, the all-powerful Father of gods and humans; Aphrodite kindled passionate desire and delight in the sensual world; Ares brought courage as well as a violence which was checked and countered by Athene, the goddess who loved both war and the peaceful crafts; Apollo, 'he who shoots from afar', was delighted by clear rationality as much as Dionysus exulted in the abandon of ecstasy. Westerners can perhaps catch a glimpse of a god-populated world in travels to India, where the faithful still pray first to Lord Ganesha, the elephant-headed guardian of the threshold and remover of obstacles, and where for many people the great pantheon of Hindu deities still minutely influences every aspect of private and public life. But on this side of the world, as Jung said: 'the Gods have become diseases; Zeus no longer rules Olympus but rather the solar plexus, and produces curious specimens for the doctor's consulting room'.[3]

Importantly, though, Jung did not mean that the energy which the old gods used to carry could now be 'cured' and set to rest. For him, the archetypes were the constant bedrock of human experience, 'the forms or riverbeds along which the current of psychic life has always flowed'. These powerful patterns that organize human experience cannot but remain 'a living system of reactions and aptitudes that determine the individual's life in invisible ways – all the more effective because invisible'.

'We think we can congratulate ourselves on having already reached such a pinnacle of clarity, imagining that we have left all these phantasmal gods far behind. But what we have left behind are only verbal spectres, not the psychic facts that were responsible for the birth of the gods. We are still as much possessed by autonomous psychic contents as if they were Olympians. Today they are called phobias, obsessions, and so forth; in a word, neurotic symptoms.'[4]

So we humans suffer if we ignore the archetypal roots of our experience and fail to honour the images by which we may intimate them. In these days, many dis-eases are on the increase in the West: the growing toll of obesity, immune disorders, depression and anxiety, anorexia and bulimia points to a profound dis-order in the basic human harmony of body and mind, matter and spirit. At the same time, the relationship between us humans and the very earth on which we live is profoundly askew, and we are reaping the devastating effects of centuries of overriding nature's balances in the search for profit. Political crises, with their cultural, national and religious divisions, threaten the safety of the world.

For many people, this dis-order of the body politic, as of the individual body and the earth itself, has become linked with an historical overemphasis on the 'masculine', discriminated consciousness which has dominated and driven the whole development of what we know as Western civilization. What for so long brought huge benefit now often seems to bring damage instead, and the past quarter of a century has seen a powerful burgeoning of a very different consciousness. The upsurge of feminism that has been building for more than 100 years has joined with a growing opposition to industrial and political practices which violate 'Mother Earth', a critique of Judeo-Christianity's systematic denigration of the feminine principle, and myriad attempts to reclaim and honour that principle. All these have brought new perspectives and strengths, but often anger, hurt and confusion as well.

In these disordered times, then, Themis, personification of the ancient feminine order which is rooted in the rhythms of the Earth herself and reaches into social patterns and individual lives, seems to carry a compensatory healing that this battered world and its inhabitants sorely need. Her *themis*, that natural law which brings together human beings and the elements of masculine and feminine just as it does the gods themselves, seems a powerful antidote to all those forces which set them against each other and tear them apart.

To understand more of what this might mean and how '*themis* energy' might be operating today in individuals, groups and societies, is not simple. The approach to psyche through ancient myths has its stout defenders. As James Hillman, foremost among them, has said: 'The Gods can't be cut off . . . they inhabit our subjectivity and govern our acts.' He returns to the saying of the Delphic oracle which was also inscribed above the lintel of Jung's house in Kusnacht: 'Whether invoked or not invoked, [the Gods] are present.' The analyst Michael Vannoy Adams also honours the gods and their tales: he has elaborated a 'mytho-psychology' based on his understanding of the 'mythological unconscious.'[5]

But some 'Jungians', let alone psychologists of other persuasions, find that approaching psyche through myth is quite problematic. Critics point out the circularity of Jung's theoretical justification: we read myths to understand more about the collective unconscious, and we assert that the collective unconscious exists through the study of myth. One interested observer from the world of social and experimental psychology has put it bluntly: 'In effect, [Jung] is telling us we need to study myth because it shows the workings of the psyche as hypothesised by him. If we reject his hypotheses about the psyche, there seems to be little reason to study myth. He needs to convince us about his model of the psyche in the first place – and by and large, most psychologists are not convinced.'[6] Objections to Jung's approach are not only theoretical, either. Most radically, the Jungian analyst Wolfgang Giegerich has insisted forcefully on myth's *irrelevance* to contemporary psychology. Recourse to myth, he argues, has become a nostalgic exercise, even a spiritual drug, which can only obscure the psychic reality that Western consciousness has decisively outgrown its mythic roots, and impede understanding of contemporary human beings and their psychological world. 'The gods have not become diseases, as Jung and Hillman wanted us to believe', says Giegerich. 'They have become *memories*, memories of former modes of being-in-the-world.'[7]

Yet, given that no archetypal energy can be fully accessible to the conscious mind, for us the metaphors of myth continue to offer a valuable way of both living with that reality and attempting to bring more of psyche into awareness. In this paradoxical endeavour, myth can help individual engagement with the deep unconscious and so with aspects of psyche intimated but as yet inaccessible to the conscious mind. As Jung said when he asked himself 'What is the myth that you are living?' he took on the search for an answer as the 'task of tasks', the way to self-understanding. So to spend time with the old stories, to become aware of which bring energy and which seem dull, to note which characters attract and which repel, can offer a way towards an individual sense of meaning. More than this, myth can bring new perspectives to the collective, both conscious and unconscious, of which individuals are a part.[8]

The task of understanding will never be complete, and the meaning of the stories will change in time and place: 'the most we can do is to dream the myth onwards and give it a modern dress.' Yet the very etymologies of the word suggest the lasting value of doing just that. 'Myth', says the mythographer Walter Otto, 'means originally the true word . . . speech about that which is.' Yet *mythos* is also related to *musteion,* which means 'to close the eyes or mouth', and is related to the English word 'mystery'. So myth becomes *the true word about that which cannot be spoken, speech about that which cannot be seen or understood.* It would be hard to find a better brief description of ego's attempt to articulate the unconscious, of the value of myth to the endeavour – or of the endeavour's final impossibility.[9]

Both the attempt and the impossibility are inevitably written into this book. Conceptually, the images and stories of Themis seem to express many qualities of the archetype that Jung called the Self.[10] This idea of an archetype of order and meaning, which is both the central focus of psyche and the force that encompasses it, which represents both the goal of psychological wholeness and the process of reaching for it, is one to which we often return. Yet because the conscious mind's attempts to express psychic totality are bound to be limited, the idea of the Self can sometimes appear abstract and removed from direct experience. We hope that by retelling the stories of Themis, and exploring '*themis* energy' at work in individual lives and collective situations, we can help to give the concept body and soul – and also add something to existing imagery. Jung knew well that his concept had its counterparts in all the great world religions. 'The self,' he said, 'is a living person and has always been there. It is an insight upon which Hindu philosophy (the equivalent of Western theology), Buddhism, Taoism, mystical Islamic sects and Christianity are all agreed.'[11] But in his writing about the Self, he drew very heavily on the symbolism of the Christian tradition, and he certainly did not turn to *feminine* embodiments of its qualities. So we hope that by exploring the imagery of a goddess rather than a god, who comes from a pre-Christian, yet still Western, tradition, we may add to a sense of what the Self is about.

The images and stories of Themis explored here speak both to the reality of a psychological force that works towards wholeness and healing and to the impossibility of giving it clear and logical expression – as well as to the central role of symbolical and mythological material in a work of bringing-to-consciousness.

This approach brings some important caveats. The first is that if the reader is looking for an academic study of Themis, they will not find it here. Instead, we relate the myths of the goddess to contemporary intimations of what we call '*themis* consciousness' as various as the minutiae of neuro-scientific research into the workings of the human organism and the flawed grandeur of the South African Truth and Reconciliation Commission. This scope seems consistent with, even demanded by, both the mythic material and psychological theory. For Jung, the Self was rooted in the body, and unless the human link to the instincts was rediscovered 'no self can come into being.' At the same time, the Self, representing as it did psychic totality, could not but encompass the collective unconscious in its cosmic entirety. Jung's understanding of the essential psychological relationship between individual and collective, through the embedding of both in the collective unconscious, is for us one of his most important contributions. Interestingly, it has also been relatively little explored, until a recent interest in 'the cultural unconscious' and the workings of 'cultural complexes' which are experienced equally by individuals and their societies. We hope that this book adds to this exploration.[12]

From the perspective of the Self as embracing both the personal and the collective, we can imagine that a lack of *themis* consciousness can bring disorder in both individuals and societies, and that the healing of each is related to the healing of the other. This understanding of the interrelationship of individuals, society and nature itself is both ancient and widespread, found in such concepts as the Chinese Tao and the Hindu *rta*. Jung's psychological expression of this ancient concept, the lifelong process of *individuation*, by which human beings become more conscious of who they are meant to be, has by definition to do with separating out a sense of individual identity from collective social norms. But this process is the very opposite of the *individualism* which seems so characteristic of contemporary Western society. 'There is,' as Jung once trenchantly put it, 'no possibility of individuation on top of Mount Everest where you are sure that nobody will ever bother you. Individuation always means relationship.' Right until the end of his life, he maintained that greater individual self-awareness had both a personal and a social purpose, and that any healing of societies and nations must begin with the individual. Instead of leading to isolating and competitive self-interest, the process of individuation would, he thought, take individuals into deeper and deeper relationship with not just other individuals but with the collective of which each is a part. And such is the nature of the collective unconscious that this relationship also extends to the whole of humankind, to whom each individual is related at the archetypal level, and even beyond, to the *unus mundus*, that 'unitary world' which brings together matter and psyche, the real and the imaginary. From this perspective of awesome responsibility, each individual's actions, thoughts and level of self-awareness must constantly influence the whole, just as the collective must influence the individual. It is precisely in this essential interplay, so it seems to us, that Themis is to be found, and her images and stories can help bridge the two.[13]

This brings the second caveat. We are concerned with archetypal dimensions in the lived experience of contemporary individuals and societies. But we are not reading myth backwards to make assertions about the lives of individuals or societies in the past. Mythology is not history, any more than dreamtime follows the laws of chronometry, and the relationship between consciousness and the unconscious changes and develops over time. So while we are concerned with the images and stories of a great and powerful ancient goddess, we are also aware that the honour paid to feminine manifestations of the divine in the ancient world seems to have had little direct correspondence to the status of actual women. To take another example: the myth of a Golden Age, when gods and humans lived together in perfect harmony, is certainly one of the most numinous and pervasive that exists, and we too return to it. But to conclude from the tellings and retellings of the myth across time and space that somewhere, sometime, such an ideal society existed, is to fall from psychology into literalism.

So mythology is not history. But mythological *patterns* can and do manifest in historical time and place. The stories of 'Diana', 'John' and 'Jennifer' (Chapters 2, 3 and 4) show how this may happen for individuals, just as the stories from the movement for restorative justice and the South African Truth and Reconciliation Commission (Chapters 7 and 8) show how it may happen for groups and even whole societies. Part of the importance of refinding the themes of ancient tales retold in modern lives lies in the way they can aid understanding of the psychological patterns which are being enacted beneath the outer action. By compensating for prevailing conscious attitudes, they may also offer intimations of other ways of being – where the 'feminine' and 'masculine' are equally honoured, for instance, or where humans live in greater harmony with 'the gods' which represent psychological elements of their common nature. Mythology is not history; but in this sense it may carry possibilities for future historical realities.

This leads to a third caveat. While we cannot know how those possibilities may unfold, what seems certain is that any coming age will be far from pure gold. Jung's 'dream of totality', to which the imagery of Themis seems to speak, is precisely that: as he insisted, wholeness is not perfection. This is what for us gives the myths of the goddess such power: they speak to a psychological capacity to contain and encompass energies which may appear dark and negative just as much as those which seem to bring light. In a world where fundamentalist forces of all sorts seek to bring different dreams of perfection into social reality, and where a dangerously usual way of dealing with opposing forces is to project into them the 'evil other', which must be sought out and destroyed, this seems of utmost relevance. To develop the psychological capacity to contain negative energies rather than to split them off into that feared and despised 'other' seems of central importance to both individuals and societies, as a preliminary to any inner or collective reconciliation and transformation.

In her work of bringing together gods and humans, the elements of the unconscious and consciousness, the stories of Themis seem consistently benign. But it is important to remember too that she is only one in a richly varied pantheon: the psychological energy that she personifies is one among many. And although she has a uniquely powerful place in that pantheon of energies, through her capacity to contain them and bring 'right order', she also has a terrifying aspect. Whenever the goddess is offended by humans who fail to observe that order, Winged Nemesis, daughter of deadly Night, will appear. Known as 'due enactment' and 'divine vengeance', Nemesis is also 'the inevitable': there is no escaping her. Her finger to her lips, she also reminds humans of what they owe to the gods and to their fellows, and her companion Shame will appear when they fail in these obligations. Whenever Tyche, goddess of fortune, heedless and whimsically scatters her bounty, Nemesis is there too, to remind humans that actions bring consequences, and if they fail in gratitude for Tyche's gift or use it ungenerously, she will chastise them.[14] Themis too, in her later manifestations as the embodiment of Justice, carries sword as well as scales, a reminder perhaps that 'divine vengeance' may also be part of her archetypal power when her 'right order' has been ignored.

In the contemporary world, it is not hard perhaps to hear the beating of Nemesis's wings as the consequences of generations of exploitation of humans, natural resources and the earth itself become ever clearer. It is not hard either to find examples of abuse in the name of Justice, or a wielding of her sword in acts of vengeance that are anything but obedient to the goddess's law. So a greater understanding of the psychological energy personified by Themis, and of her 'right order', seems the more important. The chapters of this book seek to do that first at an individual level, then through different collective examples, including one which has affected a whole society and indeed the world. Throughout, we return to the myths of Themis as the uniting thread of meaning, and through these, to an invitation to the reader's imagination to engage with the material. Jung constantly emphasized the importance of the subjective element in any reading or understanding of psychology: in this perspective, each reader will help to create a growing awareness of what 'themis consciousness' is about.

Chapter 1 introduces the goddess, and the war between Olympians and Titans, which we see as lying at the heart of many contemporary individual and collective ills. Chapters 2 and 3 illustrate this split and its healing through the story of one individual, and Chapter 4 delves into the language of the body to suggest a very basis of a universal human 'right order'. Chapter 5 is the hinge between individual and collective aspects of Themis's influence. It tells the story of Delphi, where the goddess's ancient oracle drew both private people and public representatives to a centre that was equally important to both. Such was the goddess's healing and reconciling power that Delphi drew together representatives of warring city states in search of wisdom, their enmities set aside. This holding and reconciling *themis* energy seems to be more consciously available to groups and societies today, and after introducing the lasting image of Themis as Justice in Chapter 6, Chapter 7 explores how *themis* consciousness can be seen in the contemporary development of restorative justice in many countries of the world. Chapter 8 explores how these restorative principles inspired an endeavour that involved a whole society and gave an example to the world through the work and achievements of the South African Truth and Reconciliation Commission. Chapter 9 starts with a reminder that Themis was also the one who convened the feasts of the Olympian deities, and brings to table the generosity of psychological nourishment that *themis* energy may provide.

This book began with Pamela's thesis for her analytic training programme at the C. G. Jung Institute–Boston. When Ann read it, she was excited by its ideas and implications, and particularly by the interplay between individual and collective energies with which we have both, in our previous careers and now, been seized. So she was intrigued by Pamela's invitation to cooperate in expanding the thesis into a book. We worked on all the material together, with the exception of the stories of 'Diana', 'John' and 'Jennifer', which Pamela tells. We now hope that Themis will speak to you as she has spoken to us.

Chapter 1

Birth of a goddess

Themis first appears in a story of how this world came into being, a Greek myth about the birth of the gods. Ever since storytelling began, such creation myths have told of how particular cultures explain their own genesis and nature. So they can give a picture of the dynamic psychological processes which initiate a new structure of governing cultural principles. Creation myths help peoples define themselves, they tell them what values are important. Across times and cultures, they have been recounted to young people as an essential part of their initiation into their tribe; their retelling has brought renewal at the start of the New Year; they have been evoked at times of crisis.[1] They may leave their more or less conscious traces in the lasting ceremonies of communities: the annual American rituals of Thanksgiving, for instance, are a reminder, however commercialized and half-forgotten, of that nation's beginnings and the values on which these were based.

But creation myths are also about more than the making of particular cultures and defining the place of individuals within them. Ultimately, they speak to the nature and meaning of human existence itself and its relationship to the cosmos. 'Where do I come from?' is a question that seems to be encoded into every child, and the answers can range from the most basically biological to the most loftily speculative, carrying with them other stories about the purpose of that individual life. Creation myths are never outgrown, however much other tales of other world-beginnings may follow them. Their cultural and psychological implications remain embedded in the human psyche and, as Chapters 2 and 3 explore, can still be relived in the lives of contemporary individuals.

When creation myths are viewed through Joseph Campbell's perspective, as stories about how cosmic energy has poured into human cultural manifestation, these myths also show which archetypal patterns have become powerful within a culture and which have not. Psychologically, they can indicate which energies are more readily available, and what has been repressed or lost. Helping to recover those lost aspects is the work of *themis* consciousness, as it brings together psychic contents. So first we turn to the creation myth in which Themis herself came into being, and in which so much of her Titanic inheritance was crushed by an emerging consciousness.

The poet Hesiod is thought to have written his *Theogony*, his own story of the birth of the gods, some time before 700 BCE, which makes it older than any known version of Homer's great epics *The Iliad* and *The Odyssey*.[2] It is in the *Theogony* that the goddess Themis first appears. So this is where her story must start.

In the beginning, says Hesiod, there was Chaos. Just that, nothing more.

Then out of that swirling incoherence came a shape: Gaia, Mother Earth herself, already broad and strong enough for future gods to find in her a foothold. And then came Eros, that most beautiful and irresistibly mighty power of attraction, and once Eros was there, the whole business of creation could begin. Night gave birth to Day and Space. Earth gave birth to Heaven and called him Ouranos; she made him to be her own equal, to cover her and to be a safe home for the blessed gods. Next she gave birth to the hills, and the sea.

Then Earth and Heaven together started to produce great creatures. First there were the Titans – six daughters, including Themis, and six sons. Then came the Cyclopes, strong and full of craft, guardians of thunder and lightening. They were just like the Titans, except for one curious fact: they had only one eye, right in the middle of their foreheads. But that is a detail compared with who came next: three insolent, awful creatures, the Hekatoncheires, each with 50 heads, each with 100 arms which slashed about so fast that not one could be held.

From the start, Ouranos couldn't bear his children. Every day and every night he covered Earth, and every time a child was born of this endless union he stuffed it back where it had come from, right back into Gaia's womb. He thought this a great game, he enjoyed it. And Earth? She groaned in labour and she groaned as the burden of those children grew inside her. At last she could bear it no longer. Reaching inside herself, she drew out a piece of adamant, the toughest metal of all, and honed it into a great sickle. She took no joy in what she planned, but she could see no other way to stop Ouranos's destruction of new life. Her sons liked it no better than she did; there was plenty to be afraid of in that huge, often-lowering father of theirs. But in the end crafty Kronos loved his mother and hated his father enough to seize the sickle. And when Ouranos came, accompanied by Night, to enfold Earth in his great and passionate embrace, Kronos crept from his hiding place and with that adamantine sickle cut off his father's genitals and hurled them into the sea. Ouranos howled with outrage and pain and sprang back from Earth.

Immediately all those children swarmed out, blinking in the night-light, sniffing the unaccustomed air. And then creation exploded, for good and ill alike. Joyful Love and sour Blame, the ruthless Fates and whole families of laughing water nymphs, Battles and Fights and shining stars, Glory and Lawlessness, Ruin and cleansing winds and more besides than can ever be named in a single lifetime poured from parthenogenic parents and myriad matings.

In among them all were the firstborn of Earth and Heaven, the Titans. So finally Themis, together with her brothers and sisters, was able to come into the world.[3]

This story of creation continues. But already it tells something about Themis and the world into which she arrived. She was born, finally, when Ouranos sprang back from Gaia, and that was made possible by her brother Kronos, who became known as Father Time himself. So Themis can be said to come into time, and into a specific time, when the original union of Earth and Heaven has been violently and angrily ruptured. Across times and cultures, those two great forces have come to be seen as 'the masculine' and 'the feminine' principles; most usually, as here and in, for instance, pre-Confucian China, Heaven is identified with 'the masculine' and Earth with 'the feminine'. So Themis comes into consciousness at a time of strife between masculine and feminine energies. And although the contemporary Western world may seem a long way from the one into which she and her sibling Titans emerged blinking from Mother Earth, the same psychological strife is immediately still recognizable as part of its inheritance, and as a story still played out in the lives of individual women and men.

The wave of feminism that started to break in the middle of the nineteenth century, and reached a crescendo in the last quarter of the twentieth, has brought a new level of consciousness to this ancient story, not simply socially and economically, but psychologically as well. As some women claim their 'masculine' aspect, and some men their 'feminine', it is no longer possible to make an easy equation of 'the feminine' with women and 'the masculine' with men; the very meaning of the terms is up for question, and the questioning can bring anger and bewilderment. At the same time, people in Western cultures have increasingly come to lament the dominance of the masculine and the effects of the abiding enmity between Earth and Heaven, which have come to stand too for the apparently opposing forces of feeling and reason, nature and culture. Most recently, the yearning for an equal honouring of a creative and nurturing feminine energy has fuelled not only the influential perspectives of feminism but myriad 'new' spiritualities. The very intensity of feeling conjured by and around these movements speaks to both their psychological significance and to the enormity of the rebalancing task they serve.

The legend of her birth suggests that Themis is intimately bound up with this collective psychological struggle. Appearing at that specific time when the archetypal masculine and feminine energies split apart in enmity, Themis is also, like any child, the carrier of both. This suggests that the psychological force represented by the goddess who calls the different gods together carries an important potential for reconciliation between the two. What the 'birth', the coming-to-consciousness, of Themis suggests psychologically is that *when* there is dis-order between masculine and feminine, *then* the healing energy she represents also appears. Hesiod's creation myth suggests that this dis-order is built into the unfolding of Western consciousness, part of its archetypal inheritance. But it also suggests that encoded in these mythic beginnings there is the potential to move beyond it.

Interwoven with this theme is another. Hesiod's myth suggests that the dis-order can also be seen as a differentiation necessary to psychological development: it is when Heaven and Earth, masculine and feminine, are separated that the work of creation, until then blocked in the womb of Earth, can finally begin. This necessary separation of Gaia and Ouranos has parallels in other creation myths, which suggests its archetypal nature. In ancient Egypt, for instance, the masculine principle Geb was the fertile Earth, while the feminine principle Nut stretched herself across the starry Sky to enfold all creation. But they too had to part for the work of creation to continue, and forever, says their myth, must yearn to reunite. This necessary separation of masculine and feminine can also be seen as a stage in the age-long development from an ancient world view in which the mother goddess alone was the creative source of life, death and regeneration.[4] These ancient collective unfoldings find modern expression, too, in the stories developmental psychology tells of the growth in consciousness of the individual child, from relationship only with the mother to a necessary capacity to differentiate between maternal and paternal energies.

So the separation of Heaven and Earth seems as vital to the continuing work of creation as their coming together. As Jung imagined it, these two mighty forces, the feminine principle of relatedness and the masculine principle of discrimination, are engaged in a perpetual cosmic dance: 'it is the function of Eros to unite what Logos has sundered.'[5] Yet in the unfolding of Western consciousness, that essential and equal balance has also been skewed across the generations, and creation has suffered. Hesiod's story shows how deep this goes.

For all that Kronos had cooperated with Mother Earth to release her offspring, he finally learned nothing from his own laborious and dangerous beginnings. Once he became king of the gods, he too turned on his own children, fearful of losing his power to the creative energy they would bring. One by one, as they emerged from his sister-wife Rhea, he scoffed them down, gobbling their creative potential to keep it for himself. Once more, the feminine suffered, says Hesiod, 'endless grief', until Ouranos and Gaia, now reconciled, spirited Rhea off to Crete for her latest confinement, where his grandmother took care of tiny Zeus from the moment of his birth. When Rhea came home with yet another swaddled babe, Kronos didn't even bother to look at it. So he gobbled up not a succulent little morsel but a stone. Years later, crafty Rhea brought the now glorious young Zeus home in the guise of a cup-bearer to his father. The old god, greedy as ever, had no hesitation in gulping the wine into which Rhea had mixed a powerful emetic. So he vomited up their children, and finally the next generation of gods, the Olympians, were born.[6]

But as Zeus in his turn became honoured as the father of gods and humans, once more the story of masculine dominance was repeated. Once more the father-god feared that he would be superseded by the next generation. This time, Zeus took the precaution of swallowing his pregnant wife, Metis. So the goddess Athene was born from her father's forehead. And although her mother remained in Zeus's belly, gestating the child until she forced her way into the world by becoming her father's intolerable headache, for ever after Athene has been hailed as her father's child alone. So the parthenogenic creative power of the ancient Mother Goddess becomes that of the new Father God. And a pattern becomes set, with results that reach from the realm of the gods into human lives.

As the philosopher Richard Tarnas puts it, the entire evolution of what we know as the 'Western mind' has been driven by 'a heroic impulse to forge an autonomous rational human self by separating it from the primordial unity with nature'.[7] This 'decisive masculinity' of the heroic Western mind has fundamentally affected all the religious, scientific and philosophical perspectives of Western culture for the past four millennia, and it has brought immeasurable benefits, both social and economic, philosophical and cultural. But what was once a necessary differentiation for the growth of consciousness has now become, for many, a tyranny. The cost of Western 'culture' to global nature is becoming devastatingly clear. The very word 'patriarchy' now conjures images of repression rather than a paternal force that guides its children into a welcoming world; for many, it has become a negative value judgement rather than a neutral description of a form of social organization.

In this inexorable development of Western consciousness, the dominant creation mythologies, which psychologically can be said to carry a culture's profoundest sense of what human beings are about, have been of universes ruled by increasingly powerful gods. Hesiod's version of creation arrives at a cusp. In his world, Zeus is indisputably the father who rules both gods and humankind. But the alliances on Olympus are by no means always forged along same-sex lines. There is a recognition of both masculine and feminine strengths; Hera constantly chides her husband Zeus with the reminder that she too has been a great deity in her own right. The gods and goddesses, bidden together by Themis, can still enjoy each other and the great feasts that she prepares.

Yet already there has been an important shift in Themis's power and the relationship between masculine and feminine forces. Another ancient story looks back to a time when the Olympians were not yet enthroned, but struggling to establish their supremacy over the old deities of whom she was one. The *Homeric Hymn to Apollo* tells of how Themis's ancient oracular voice at Delphi, the centre of the known world, was usurped when Olympian Apollo murdered her protective serpent Python and took the oracle for himself: the wisdom that came from Mother Earth herself was annexed by the very personification of rational mind. This story, which is explored in Chapter 5, has striking parallels with the Babylonian creation myth, the *Enuma Elish*, first inscribed some time before 1500 BCE. And that epic is decisive, for in it, for the first time, the great Mother Goddess who generates creation as part of herself is replaced by a god who 'makes' creation as something separate. More than that, creation is 'made' not as an expression of the life force itself, but out of inert matter: the lasting separation of the realms of mind and body begins. In the *Enuma Elish*, the triumphant and violent murder of the great serpent goddess Tiamat by Marduk, 'wisest of the gods', and his subsequent re-creation of the universe out of her dead body, the dominant Judeo-Christian mythology of Western culture would find its roots.[8]

In the biblical Genesis creation myth, as in Hesiod's, the creation of Night and Day is followed by the separation of Heaven and Earth. But from the start, the two explanations of the world's beginnings – and so the two ideas of what human beings are about – could not be more different. In Genesis, the creative force which was once stored in Gaia, Mother Earth herself, belongs to the uniquely powerful God. Human beings are part of his great creation of the universe and all that is in it, products not of nature but of a supreme spirit. The radical differentiation between mind and matter, Heaven and Earth, 'masculine' and 'feminine', is there from the start, and very soon the supremacy of the first is underlined. The story of the Fall, of how the first humans forfeited the favour of God through the fault of woman beguiled by the serpent of evil, has had the most profound and lasting effect on every aspect of Western human endeavour and organization, and on individual as well as collective understandings and relationships. From that moment on, human beings were no longer an intrinsic part of the natural world, living in harmony with its laws. The opposition between 'nature' and 'culture' was wound up: 'Cursed is the ground because of you,' God tells Adam, 'in toil you shall eat of it all the days of your life; / thorns and thistles it shall bring forth to you;/ and you shall eat the plants of the field. / In the sweat of your face/ you shall eat bread' (Genesis 3: 17–19). The opposition between 'masculine' and 'feminine' was wound up too, as God puts Eve, 'the Mother of all Living', under Adam's rule. The serpent, once a manifestation of the goddess herself, is crushed: 'Because you have done this,/ cursed are you above all cattle/ and above all wild animals;/ upon your belly you shall go,/ and dirt you shall eat / all the days of your life. I will put enmity between you and the woman, /and between your seed and her seed; / he shall bruise your head, / and you shall bruise his heel' (Genesis 3: 14–15).

From these beginnings, the earthly and material world became conflated with woman herself as the source and seat of both human weakness and human sin. St Augustine put his mighty theological seal on this understanding of the inferiority of the entire realm of the feminine in the fourth century CE, when in his *City of God* he chastised those who hold that God is the soul and the earth the body, with its corollary that 'there is nothing in earth that is not part of God'. This would mean, he argues, that every time a man trod upon the earth he trod part of God under his feet, and every time he killed a living creature, he would be killing part of the Deity. He found the idea appalling: 'I will not relate what others may think of it. I cannot speak it without exceeding shame.' This secularization of the natural world has brought a profound and lasting legacy at many levels, from the wholesale exploitation of earth's resources and disrespect for its laws, to understandings of the nature of woman herself. Eight centuries after Augustine, St Thomas Aquinas, the greatest medieval theologian, was teaching that woman is in her very nature and physical substance *ignobilior et vilior* than man, a falling away from the 'true', male human being who is made in God's image, superior precisely because in him 'the discretion of reason predominates'. The echoes of this teaching, which go back to the Genesis creation myth, have reverberated through the centuries to affect both women and men. As the psychologist James Hillman has roundly put it: 'The psychological history of the male–female relationship in our civilisation may be seen as a series of footnotes to the tale of Adam and Eve.'[9]

What place for the Titans, firstborn of Earth and Heaven, in this fallen world? The mythic universe described by Hesiod has long been superseded in Western consciousness. But the old tales do not die: they remain encoded to tell of the wealth of other archetypal patterns, and to offer other possibilities for being. These ancient gods, which were 'born' before Olympian consciousness, seem to represent instinct, intense emotion, physical processes – that whole realm which would later be despised and feared as 'inferior' to the rational powers of mind. Their name means simply 'Lord', and they have their own laws, as any of us may discover each time we are swept up in a thought or action which seems bewilderingly and even frighteningly alien to our conscious mind and self-understanding. Their kingdom is that of all the powerful and seemingly irrational aspects of the body and psyche on which human nature, both individual and collective, must irrevocably rest. An ancient legend underlines this: as we shall see, some said that the human race itself was born from their ashes.[10]

So the psychological energies which the Titans embody remain part of the human heritage. Yet in the long development of Western consciousness, it has been consistently difficult to allow these a place. Originally, some say, there were 14 Titans, not 12, and they ruled over the seven planets, two over each, and so brought together the realms of Heaven and Earth, their own parents. But to the early Christians, keenly tormented by the opposition of spirit and matter, the Titans' instinctual realm was anathema, and Christian doctrine denied their heavenly paternity. It often called them 'earth-born Giants', with all the negative connotations that would bring, and taught that it was their lustful unions with the daughters of men which had caused God to despair of his whole human project, and send his mighty cleansing flood. These 'earth-born' creatures were inevitably linked with the apparent grossness of the body and the material world. In the twelfth century, for instance, Bernardus of Chartres was explaining that the Giants declare war on God 'when bodies oppress knowledge and virtue'; they are defeated 'when bodies are mortified'.

These old gods seemed also to embody that pride which twentieth-century psychologists would come to identify as 'titanic' inflation: the Giants were also identified with Lucifer and his rebel angels, cast from Heaven for their overweening presumption into the deepest places of Hell.[11]

This was not the first time that the Titans had been consigned to the darkest depths, not the first time that an attempt had been made, in psychological terms, to repress their energies into the deep unconscious. Zeus hated them as a threat to his own dynasty. His decade-long war against them was long and bitter – an image of the beginnings of the painful struggle between mind and matter, the rational and the irrational, with which Western culture has lived ever since. For a long stretch of the war, the forces were evenly matched. The balance only tipped in Zeus's favour when grandmother Gaia suggested that he enlist the fearsome Hekatoncheires, the ones with all those heads and flailing arms, whom their father Ouranos had kept imprisoned for so many years. Strengthened by hatred for their father (again!) and by the nectar and ambrosia which Zeus poured down their throats to seal the contract, the Hekatoncheires readied themselves for the most terrible battle of the war. Heaven itself let out a great groan when Zeus launched his flashing stream of thunderbolts and blinding lightning; earth and sea roared terribly as they boiled in the fire, and the intensity of the heat reached Chaos itself. That is just the start of what it took to conquer the Titans. And this is what it took to imprison them in the deepest realms of Tartarus, which lies as far below earth as earth below heaven: 300 stones, hurled by the Hekatoncheires' 300 gigantic hands, a wall of bronze and round that again a triple layer of darkest Night, all beneath the very roots of earth and sea. And there those three Hekatoncheires still live – guards on whose loyalty Zeus can rely.[12]

There the Titans were left, too, and for some there their story ends, their only function, as the mythographer Kerenyi puts it, to be defeated – and so emphasize the superiority of the gods who succeeded them. Yet psychologically, their energy lives on, and like any energy which is repressed and imprisoned, as Zeus imprisoned the Titans themselves, it will be perceived in its negative form. One further legend speaks to this, and it has to do with the very elements of human nature. The reason that the Titans finally were consumed by fire, their ashes gathered up to make the human race, was, some say, because they were thunderbolted by Zeus in the act of consuming his young son Dionysus. In this tale, the Titans had managed to escape from the underworld. Their faces whitened like ghosts, they seized the playing boy, dismembered him, cast the seven pieces into a cauldron and, when they were boiled, began to roast them on seven spits. Some even say they had eaten all but the heart by the time the wrathful Zeus destroyed them and ordered the remembering of his son.[13]

This story can be read as further confirmation of the gross brutality of the old Titanic forces as it appears to a later consciousness which must repress and finally destroy their power. Yet the ritualistic nature of the Titans' act – the whitened faces, the seven spits and seven pieces corresponding to the seven planets over which these old deities once had rule – may suggest something else: a sacrifice which in psychological terms has to do with seeking to ingest the qualities of the sacrificed. Dionysus was to become honoured as the deity of the ecstasy of the irrational; he moved particularly among woman, and in the instinctual, natural world. So although his qualities, which came into being at the later stage of Olympian consciousness, might seem very different from those of the Titans, their ways and his might not be so very distant after all. But while Dionysus was revered, the Titans were cast out. So their capture and sacrifice of the boy may also be read as an attempt by these old gods to regain recognition, to reclaim some of the honour he now inspired.

Yet for all we humans were born from the Titans' ashes, they are hardly remembered now. In the continuing development of Western consciousness their once awesome power has been depotentiated over the centuries until now they are no more than the the the blundering and stupid giants of fairy tale and pantomime, always outwitted by the hero from a younger, wilier generation. But in psychological reality, a happy ending seems much less likely, Titanic power less easily destroyed. Repressed psychic contents do not go away. Instead, they are released into the world to be unconsciously played out, their power projected on to enemy 'others', whether individuals or collectives, rather than being responsibly owned; or they are buried deep in individual bodies, producing incapacitating symptoms and dis-eases.

In the prevailing Western myth of progress, both have happened. The Titans have come to represent that 'brute force' which 'civilization' needs to overcome and grow beyond. They have left no rituals through which consciousness can connect to them, and so they have become, as the mythographer Kerenyi puts it, simply 'savage beings, subject to no laws'. There is nothing noble or fine about them: low cunning and deceitfulness are the qualities they are known for. And if they succeed, then nothing good is likely to come of it. These days, the very word 'Titanic' conjures an image of a colossal luxury liner sunk by an iceberg on its maiden voyage – a powerful warning against the overreaching arrogance that sees 'civilized' technology as able to conquer nature to make the world its own. The 'titanic inflation' that is projected on to the old gods is still part of human nature and human affairs, thundering through local economies in the destructive gigantism of multinational corporations, voraciously gobbling the earth's bounty in the insatiable appetite for profit. So gigantic, so titanic, has this appetite become that wounded nature itself is turning more and more its own destructive face: earthquakes and hurricanes are a warning we still seem not to heed, and global warming threatens human life. Human greed is a huge force, and it can seem, as Jungian analyst Raphael Lopez-Pedraza says, that 'the challenge posed to an individual consciousness by the Titanic collective can only increase.'[14]

Yet the opposition between a Titanic collective and heroic individual consciousness may itself be part of a myth of progress, another story of Jack the Giant-Killer. That myth is beginning to look a little threadbare in light of today's realities, and its shadow qualities are becoming more apparent. The cost of 'progress' now seems dangerously high and the 'heroic' often seems to shade into a destructive individualism. From this perspective, the war between Olympians and Titans is bound to be profoundly damaging both to individuals and to the societies to which they belong, as both expression and perpetuation of the opposition in the Western psyche between mind and body, spirit and matter, culture and nature. And like many wars, the longer it is perpetuated, the more entrenched it becomes and the more destructive the weapons it employs. At first, it carried to a new generation the theme that had been played out ever since that first enmity between Heaven and Earth; it had already become more complex as the original two protagonists became the 12 old gods ranged against the 12 new ones. Today, the complexities have become immeasurably greater and the weapons of our own potential mass destruction that the Olympians can deploy have become hugely more complex too, not just technologically but intellectually.

Much of modern psychology has been based on Freud's perception of the human psyche as divided against itself, the forces of the rational ego embattled against the brute instincts of the id on one hand and the repressions of the superego on the other. For him, it was the task of psychoanalysis to strengthen the heroic ego – 'where id was, there shall ego be.'[15] From these beginnings has grown the popular ego-psychology that insists that 'anyone can do anything' if only they set their rational mind to it. Yet still the extraordinary achievements of the Western mind seem increasingly to leave individual Western bodies, just as much the body of the earth herself, dis-ordered and suffering in ways which suggest that the value of the old enmities has run its course. The Olympian efforts that have gone into keeping the Titanic instinctual energy imprisoned have not just failed, but turned the Titans, as any repressed energy, to showing their destructive face. It seems time to try another way.

Jung's view of the way humans work was very different from that of Freud. From early on, he was preoccupied by the relationship between the archetypes which are for him the basis of the human psyche – and so consciousness and spirit – and the instincts which are the motor force in humans just as any animal species. From the start he saw these forces not as enemies but as 'correlates' which together made up the collective unconscious, and he very often lamented the way in which the Western mind had split them apart and lost touch with its instinctual roots. For him, both were aspects of the same 'vital activity' that accounted for the psychology of human beings. Although archetype and instinct might seem 'the most polar opposites imaginable', they existed side by side in the human creature: 'Man finds himself simultaneously driven to act and free to reflect.' And fundamentally, it was in their nature not to fight but, as all opposites, to draw together.[16]

As time went on, Jung saw less and less opposition between archetype and instinct. 'The archetypes are simply the forms which the instincts assume,' he said, and he came to see them as both 'images and emotions' *and* 'systems of readiness for action . . . inherited with the brain structure'. Finally, he understood psyche and matter as two different aspects of the same fundamental reality, the unitary world, the *unus mundus*. Although this would always be unknowable in its totality, Jung foresaw that the future work of human consciousness would be to reunite what the Western mind had split apart. For individuals already, he saw that relationship with the instincts was an essential prerequisite to the work of individuation, that process by which human beings become more fully who they are meant to be. The task of psychotherapy was to preserve or restore the unity and totality of the individual, and in this endeavour, balance between instinct and rationality was essential. To favour the first led to 'chaos and nihilism' and the destruction of the unity of the individual; to favour the second led to even more far-reaching consequences, the 'disorientation and fragmentation' of society itself. In the search of greater balance between instinct and rationality, unconscious and consciousness, the potential for healing was built into the very structure of human beings, in the pre-existing unity of the myriad world of the archetypes: in attention to archetypal images, the emotions they engender and the actions to which they drive, that potential may come nearer to realization.[17]

In the work towards healing the split between Titans and Olympians which seems so urgent for both individuals and societies, it is the archetypal image and energy personified by Themis that above all seems to carry the potential for reconciliation. She herself was a Titan and yet she became greatly honoured by the Olympians: so the energy she represents has to do with bringing together the two. Born of Earth and Heaven, the primordial 'feminine' and 'masculine', she unites the energies and meanings of both. She represents a principle of natural order more ancient than the rule of Olympus, which suggests that the irrational world of instincts and emotions, far from being a 'savage' realm, 'subject to no laws', has an order of its own, to which her legends may be a guide. And that order is powerful enough, the stories tell, to hold together the disparate energies of the Olympians and humans as well.

How is this reconciling energy, this *themis* consciousness, to be further understood? The next two chapters trace the way the energy flowed through the analysis of one individual, as she worked to bring together the world of intellect and her repressed instincts. The first step towards dialogue between the two, however, is to unlock those dark fastnesses of Tartarus rather than attempting vainly to prevent the Titans' inevitable escapes – to try to become more conscious of those forces buried in the deep unconscious rather than to repress them. The work of unlocking is what the next chapter is about.

Chapter 2

The return from Tartarus

As far below the earth as the earth is below the heavens, 300 stones on top of them, a wall of bronze and triple layer of darkest Night surrounding them: Zeus was taking no chances when he locked the Titans into darkest Tartarus and left those mighty Hekatoncheires to guard their escape. But psychological contents are not so easily repressed. The tendency of opposites seems to be to draw together in conscious awareness, rather than remaining split apart. This fuller consciousness seems to be psyche's purpose.

So the Titans have continued to insist on attention and, despite the Olympians' best locksmiths, escape from Tartarus time and again – sometimes to cause suffering and chaos when their claims are denied, sometimes to appear more benignly when their place in the scheme of things is acknowledged. The ancient Greeks knew the importance of paying them respect. Even as Zeus was honoured and feared as father of gods and humans, the reign of his father, the Titan Kronos, was remembered as the Golden Age – the time when human beings lived like gods themselves, their happy hearts untroubled by work or sorrow or illness, when fertile Mother Earth gave her fruits unasked and death came gentle as a sleep. From that golden time there had never been anything but decline, down to the harshness of the Age of Iron. But even now Kronos was remembered and revered: some said that while his son ruled Olympus, he still ruled the Isles of the Blessed, where the favourites of the gods live in everlasting bliss.[1]

In those ancient times, when the gods and goddesses were still known to the conscious psyche, life was alive with the experience of Titans and Olympians, body and mind, nature and spirit. During the time of Homer, these dualities were held together, both known as aspects of soul. One was *psyche*, which is the soul manifested by the breath – the spirit-soul. This is the aspect which has survived today, first having taken flight to Mount Olympus and then into the transcendent Judeo-Christian world of the spirit. But for the ancients, there was another soul, and this was known as *thymos* (also translated as *thumos*), the soul that is manifested by the passions. *Thymos* was experienced as an inner wisdom coming from the emotions or the instincts, often associated with the heart or the midriff.[2] There are no English words that adequately describe what *thymos* represents today, but its connection with the heartfelt passions has been translated by one author as the *blood-soul*, or the *heart-soul*.[3] This is the soul of immanence, the soul that speaks to us from the body, and it is experienced very differently from the soul of transcendence that calls to us from afar. Even though, paradoxically, everyone must intimate its existence, through those 'gut feelings' and the blood that boils in rage or runs cold in fear, the living connection with this soul has been lost. Its unique language and vocabulary have been lost along with its name, and are only now, as Chapter 4 explores, beginning to be understood and valued.

The notion of two souls has been known across cultures and down the ages, in a continuing search to express the complexity of being human. In ancient Egypt, for instance, the two souls were the individual *ba*, and the greater *ka*, 'the mother', or universal life force in which all creation was held, and to which the individual soul returned after death. More directly, the concept of blood-soul and spirit-soul is analogous in Western antiquity with *eros* and *logos*; in the Chinese tradition with *yin* and *yang*, and in Christianity with body and spirit. All these great pairings have also included the fundamental differentiation between 'feminine' (*eros, yin*, body) and 'masculine' (*logos, yang*, spirit). But there is a crucial difference between the first two and the third: whereas *logos* and *eros* and *yin* and *yang* are complementary, equally essential elements in the great dance of creation, the Christian tradition came to see body and spirit as antagonists rather than vital partners. In its denigration of the body and the feminine, it is the connection with the blood-soul which has suffered most. The whole realm of the emotions and instincts, long associated with 'the feminine', has been devalued.

But the claims of the blood-soul have remained insistent, and the struggle of Goethe's Faust is one that many people would still recognize today:

> Two souls, alas, are housed within my breast,
> And each will wrestle for the mastery there.
> The one has passions craving crude for love,
> And hugs a world where sweet senses rage;
> The other longs for pastures fair above,
> Leaving the mark for lofty heritage.[4]

Yet importantly, alongside this struggle of opposites, there is also a desire for their reconciliation – the psychological energies that push apart and bring together seem equally to be built into the nature of the human being. Alongside Christian teachings on the opposition of spirit and matter, for instance, there also ran an underground desire for, and work towards, their reunion. Across Europe, right through from the twelfth century until the end of the seventeenth and beyond, alchemists sought to transform base matter into gold. This insistent search – which drew no less a scientist than Sir Isaac Newton to its service – was not only a material one. The 'uncommon gold' which many alchemists sought was a spiritual understanding of 'the miracles of one thing' – the fundamental unity of matter with spirit. For these alchemists, the old god Saturn – the Titan Kronos with his Roman name – represented the *prima materia*, the essential material with which they toiled and prayed through their arcane texts and baffling experiments; this was also, mysteriously, the goal of the work, the 'uncommon gold', or philosopher's stone, itself. As one alchemical text, the *Splendor Solis*, emphasized, the work also had to do with the essential unity between inner and outer – and so between individuals and the world as well: 'Study what thou art/ . . . All that is without thee/Also is within. Amen.'[5]

The arcane quest of the alchemists, which Jung saw as a metaphorical precursor of his own understanding of psychic functioning, was far from that of ordinary people. Yet for them too, the Titans remained lastingly alive. Official Christian doctrine, as the last chapter shows, demonized them as Giants. But those giants, fight them as the fairy-tale heroes might, refused to go away: they remained part of the fairy world of ghosts, sleeping heroes, ancestral spirits and old gods which coexisted with official Christianity. This was a world which could be glimpsed round every dimly lit corner well into the eighteenth century and beyond. It could bring both terror and comfort – the very word 'fairy' has its roots in *fata*, goddess of destiny and fate, against whose dictates human beings are powerless, and in Middle English *feyen*, which means to unite, to bind. So human beings are bound inescapably to their instincts, fated to carry their Titanic selves in a nature in which blood-soul and spirit-soul are inseparable. Time was when this unity was honoured, and the price for struggling against it was known. In the Middle Ages, when for most people spirit and matter still worked as a mysterious whole, the penalty for ignoring this could bring on 'fairy', a *bodily* disease of *spiritual* origin which could only be cured by *spiritual* means.[6]

Reason's increasing dominance over the instinctual realm weakened this perception of the essential connection between spirit and matter; centuries passed before the insights of depth psychology and psychosomatic medicine recalled it, and so kept open one path towards healing the Olympian–Titanic split. But that split has been deepening for a long while. Even by the time that Titania became Shakespeare's Queen of the Fairies in his *Midsummer Night's Dream*, only her name remained to recall the once great origins of her kingdom. Her husband, King Oberon, had been demonized by the prevailing culture until only wizards recognized him and evoked his power. By now too, the realm of giants and fairies was quite literally diminished: Titania's subjects were so tiny that they staggered under the weight of a bee's honey-sack. Even now, however, something of the old Titanic power remained: the spells of the fairy world could still transport the young lovers into a forest of darker, fiercer passions that were as much part of them as their Athenian sophistication. But finally, Olympian order was restored. For rational King

Theseus, the enchanted happenings of that midsummer's night were merest fantasy, the sort of thing dreamed up by lovers, poets and madmen.[7]

Over four centuries later, the individual and collective suffering caused by the Titan–Olympian split does not take much seeking. To heal it by containing those powerful opposites now seems to be an urgent individual and collective task. But how do we recognize the split, and how might it be healed? This healing is the work of *themis* consciousness, and the story of Diana offers a striking illustration of how this might operate, which speaks not just for her and other individuals, but for the culture too. The story is the more striking because neither Diana nor her analyst had any conscious idea of Themis, her legends or her attributes. It was only some two years after their work together had ended that Pamela, in her own explorations of the goddess, realized how Themis's stories had been retold through Diana's own, and how the psychological force that the goddess personifies, which this book calls *themis* energy and *themis* consciousness, had been the healing factor.

Diana

When Diana first came into analysis, she was 25 years old and studying for a Master's degree in English while working as an editor for a publishing house. She was attractive and appeared intensely present in the session. Although her attention had a hypervigilant quality, she was articulate and intelligent, with an agile and analytical mind. Diana said that she was seeking therapy because she was having episodes of dissociation and hallucinations. This was quite striking, since her polished demeanour would never have suggested such suffering. When asked what she meant by hallucinations, she said that under certain circumstances she would see images outside herself that turned into frightening beings. Then she would become terrified. She described a recent incident where the images overcame her, and her boyfriend had needed to hold her for hours until she calmed down. When this happened, she felt overwhelming disgust for how out of control her emotional self had become. She said that the episodes began when she was a child, and when they first appeared, she turned them into monsters to try to scare herself even more, so that she could teach herself not to be afraid of them. This worked for a while, but then the images took on a life of their own. In later years, Diana had even tried cutting or injuring herself, 'to bring herself back to earth'.

To try to understand why these episodes had begun, Diana was asked to describe her early family life. She told a tale of suffering and conflict. Her Jewish father and Italian mother had married in defiance of their families, and appeared to be each other's opposites. Her father was a cold and controlling businessman and her mother was emotional and demanding. They soon found themselves in destructive battles, but decided to have a child to try to hold the marriage together. Diana was born, but her parents divorced before she was one year old. Her first mission in life became a failure – a fact that her mother never let her forget.

Diana lived with her mother, whose chaotic life was overwhelming and emotionally destructive for her daughter. As she got older, Diana became more and more defiant, and this led her mother to abuse her verbally and beat her. She was often left with her mother's parents, and received some nurturing from her grandmother. But between the ages of five and seven, she was sexually abused by her grandfather, and the terrifying images and constant nightmares began. Later, Diana learned that her mother had also been sexually abused by her own father. Yet she had nevertheless left her daughter with him during the child's early, most vulnerable years.

When Diana was 11, her father obtained custody of her, because of the horrendous conditions in which she was being raised. When she moved in with him and his new wife, she began to have a sense of stability for the first time. But her father was very demanding and controlling, and pushed her to excel. If she tried to express her emotions, they were discounted, and labelled as 'Diana's problems'. Diana eventually decided that she was only Jewish, and began to hate her 'Italian' side, blaming it for the emotional and seemingly irrational part of her personality.

So when Diana began analysis, she had these two distinct worlds: one was terrifying and overwhelming, and the other rational and analytical. Instinct and affects, feared as the experience of her intrusive and devouring mother and grandfather, had been severed in her psyche by her father's cool rationality, which is also the dominant way of being in contemporary Western culture. In the language of the myths and archetypes, the Titans had certainly been buried. But Diana's analytical consciousness was becoming less and less successful at keeping them in Tartarus. As yet, however, there was no dialogue between the Titan and Olympian aspects of her psyche, and she had very little sense of a stable and secure self that could mediate between these extremes. She was terrified of her instinctual nature, her blood-soul, and sought to suppress it. She tried to identify with the more cognitive and rational spirit-soul, as personified by her father. But her blood-soul rebelled, causing overwhelming affect, and even drove her into cutting herself – perhaps an unconscious attempt to make the blood connection she so desperately needed.

As happens in so many relationships, opposites attract – at least initially. Diana's mother and father had found themselves drawn to each other with the sort of unconscious intensity celebrated in the most passionate poetry and prose. The mother's Titanic emotion was just what the cool Olympian father needed to become more whole, and the explosive, uncontained mother needed the bounded rationality that Diana's father could provide. But as often happens too, neither partner used the experience of the other to become more whole. Poised on the eve of a 'ten-year war between the Titans and the Olympians', they did what Ouranos and Gaia, and Kronos and Rhea did so many thousands of mythological years before them. They gave birth to a child in the hopes that this third thing, a small innocent child, would do what they were unable to do for themselves, and bring together the opposites as they could not. This placed a huge burden on the newly born Diana. For her, as for myriad children like her, the unresolved psychological tasks of the parents were left for the child to take up as her unconscious fate. As Jung said, 'nothing exerts a stronger psychic effect upon the human environment, and especially upon children, than the life which the parents have not lived'.[8]

For Diana's parents, the task of reclaiming their unlived lives was too great: each demonized the other, and their marriage did not hold. The child, torn between two extremes, was first thrown into the realm of a Titanic mother and grandfather. After years of fending for herself as best she could, she was taken to live with her Olympian father where she was taught to act as though her Titanic emotions did not exist.

So Diana arrived at analysis with the burden of her parents' unlived lives, as well as unconsciously living the psychological and mythological drama of the buried Titans and the repressed blood-soul. Her psyche seemed to be a place where individual and cultural trauma had merged. This became even more clear when she presented a picture (Figure 2.1) that she had drawn months before beginning analysis, during a time of extreme distress.

When Diana brought this picture into analysis, she was not able to say much at all about what it represented to her; she only knew that it pleased her in some way. Symbolic material, as it appears in pictures or dreams, comes from a place in the psyche beneath rational waking consciousness. One analyst has described this place as an oracular source, comparable to the ancient oracles like the one at Delphi.[9] Jung described it as the Self, which both represents the totality of psychological wholeness and fuels the process of reaching towards it: although we can never know this place entirely, the images which appear from it help to balance the conscious attitude and reconcile splits between the conscious mind and the unconscious. This work of balancing and reconciliation is the realm of Themis, who, as Chapter 5 explores, was for so long herself the oracle of Delphi: it is *themis* energy which brings together different psychological aspects in a movement towards greater wholeness.

It is not surprising that Diana had few words to say about her drawing, since so much in it represented what she had spent years trying to repress. The chaotic images in the upper left, the dripping blood, the intertwined masks of tragedy and the caution about killing and destruction: together these present an image of the repressed and unknown blood-soul whose force in Diana's psyche was finally being seen. But importantly, her picture also shows, amid all the psychic dispersion, a powerful balance to her rational consciousness. The images of the two 'snakewomen' and the woman whose hands are dripping in blood show that Diana has already unconsciously made the necessary blood connection, although she is still merged in figure and form with the archetypal snake energies.

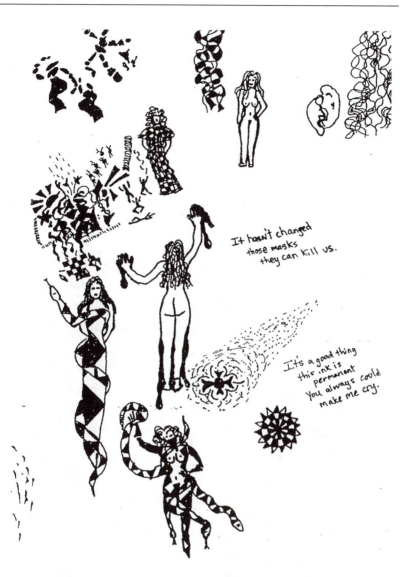

Within the image: "It hasn't changed those masks they can kill us."

"It's a good thing this ink is permanent you always could make me cry."

Figure 2.1 Emergence of the blood-soul.

These energies carry ancient power. Diana's 'snakewomen' immediately bring to mind time-honoured connections. The story of Eve and the defiled snake from the Garden of Eden is the West's prime example of how 'snake-women' and their power have been denigrated and repressed; the tale of Themis and her slain protector-serpent Python from Delphi, which is told in Chapter 5, underlines the pervasiveness of this theme in Western culture. Yet in Diana's picture, that serpent power is also rehonoured, and her images are a reminder that some of the earliest and most lasting representations of the primordial goddess take serpentine form. Already in the Neolithic civilization of Old Europe, between about 7000 and 3500 BCE, a major manifestation of the goddess was as 'Lady Snake', Mistress of the Lower Waters, who brings life to vegetation from beneath the earth. This enduring image finds particularly striking representation in the 'snakewoman' on the left of Diana's drawing, which uncannily echoes the serpent-entwined Roman goddess Atargatis (Figure 2.2). Originally a Syrian fertility goddess, here Atargatis wears an Egyptian-style headdress – one indication perhaps of the spread of her power. This image also brings another connection with Themis: her daughter Astraea, who carries the goddess's justice into human institutions and whom we meet in Chapter 6, is also entwined with Atargatis in legend's unfolding. And as the snake-goddess still emerges from the serpent's jaws in a

Figure 2.2 The timeless serpent energy: in Roman Atargatis (Museo Nazionale). ALINARI Archives, Florence.

contemporary folk image from India (Figure 2.3), it seems that the power of the image is limited by neither time nor space.[10]

Psychologically, the snake and serpent can represent – as the ancient worshippers of Lady Snake already seemed to intimate – libido or the life force, and regeneration. For Jung, it also symbolized the centre of the instincts and its connection with the body and the sympathetic nervous system. This instinctive centre receives information from organs such as the heart, stomach,

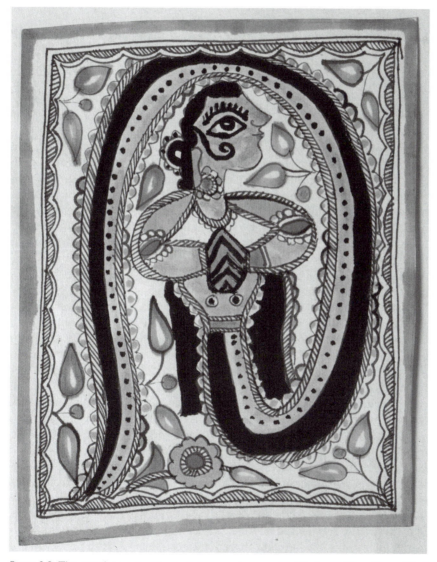

Figure 2.3 The timeless serpent energy: a contemporary Hindu goddess from Bihar. Author's collection.

lungs, kidneys, and intestines, and Jung connected it with the blood-soul too. He believed that nothing of importance should be decided without considering this centre, and recommended sleeping on the matter, 'for in sleep, consciousness is extinct and there you have a chance to become acquainted with the reaction of the serpent'. A serious deviation in the functioning of the instinctive centre could, he thought, 'risk a grave disturbance in our glandular organs or in our *blood circulation*'. And he was convinced that if our consciousness is not in practically the same tune or rhythm as this lower centre, 'under particularly unfavourable conditions one can be killed'.[11]

Diana's unconscious seemed to validate this. In her picture, the following phrase appeared:

> It hasn't changed
> those masks
> they can kill us.

Diana had no rational explanation for these words, saying only that they had appeared in poem form from somewhere other than her conscious mind. Symbolically, however, masks often refer to the aspect of the psyche that Jung calls the persona, itself the Latin word for the masks worn by actors in classical drama. For Jung, the persona is the way in which we relate to the world, a system of adaptation to its demands, and as such important and necessary if we are to find ease as social beings. The danger, however, is that the demands of others can create too rigid a mask, which stifles the wealth of other aspects of being, and makes for a two-dimensional existence.[12] Diana's mask was one of cool rationality, which was originally imposed on her by her father. She herself, however, also embraced this, when she decided that she was 'only Jewish', and rejected her 'Italian side' as representing all she feared and hated in the realm of the emotions. But psyche began to insist on a healing of that split. Diana presented a strong and powerful persona to the world, but was often overwhelmed by unconscious snake energies. Her reasoned and analytical persona was not in touch with her deeper instinctual serpent self, and through her drawing, the unconscious was letting her know that things were reaching a point where this could be quite dangerous.

Diana knew nothing of the imagery of the goddess, and was not able to make any conscious connection with her own snake-energy. Since she had lost her connection with the blood-soul and the language it speaks, she found it impossible to put into words what happened to her when her hallucinations and dissociations were triggered. So she was encouraged to continue to make drawings that expressed how she felt during the times of extreme distress. One of them (Figure 2.4) imaged how she felt before and during one of her terrifying hallucinations. She brought this after an extremely disturbing experience with her family one Christmas.

The picture's undifferentiated mass of heads, bodies, and arms gave visual

Figure 2.4 Images of dissociation.

form to a range of expressions, emotions and affects, and represented the types of images that Diana saw in her hallucinations. For her, these were overwhelming and terrifying, and she had no way to relate to them or incorporate them into her consciousness. But what is striking is that this picture can also be seen as her psyche's image of the Hekatoncheires, those many-headed and many-armed children of Ouranos and Gaia, who guard the opening to Tartarus that leads to where the Titans are buried. Nearly 3000 years after Hesiod wrote his *Theogony*, Diana's psyche came up with an image much like his, of the guardian of the buried and repressed Titanic forces.

This psychological barrier is often found among people who have suffered trauma. It can feel impenetrable, limiting or even preventing connection between individuals and causing pain and suffering for the individual who is divided against himself or herself. Many psychological schools label the barrier 'psychopathology', and describe it in terms of splitting, identification, idealization, trance states, switching among multiple centres of identity, depersonalization, and psychic numbing. Essentially, however, the barrier is a defender of the trauma-shaken psyche of the individual, as it was for Diana against the buried Titanic emotions that seemed so negative and threatening.

The damage done by abuse in childhood can be profound. Developmental neuropsychiatrists have even shown that there can be a constellation of brain abnormalities associated with it. Through the use of the electroencephalogram (EEG), functional magnetic resonance imaging (fMRI), and developmental testing on individuals with histories of psychiatric distress and abuse as well as on so-called 'normal subjects', researchers have been able to show that the abused individuals had arrested development in the left hemisphere of the brain. They also had smaller middle portions of the corpus collosum (the primary pathway connecting the two hemispheres), and abnormalities in the cerebellar vermis (the middle strip between the two hemispheres of the brain), which appears to play an important role in emotional and attentional balance and regulates electrical activity within the limbic system. Interestingly, this research also found that males with a history of neglect in childhood and females with a history of sexual abuse were the most affected.[13]

This work suggests that the childhood abuse of Diana – and of others with similar experiences – may have created a literal block between the hemispheres of their brains, which could well be imaged as the Olympians stuffing the Titans into Tartarus and so powerfully blocking their escape. The Hekatoncheires appeared in mythical form in Hesiod's tale as the representative of a culture's burial of its 'Titanic' aspects and the splitting of blood-soul from spirit-soul. They also appeared in Diana's drawing when the impact of her trauma threatened to overwhelm her. We can only speculate about the impact that the cultural abuse of the feminine and the blood-soul over the millennia may have had on human brain development, and about the enormity of the work that may have to be done to recover psychic balance between blood-soul and spirit-soul.

The neuropsychiatrists involved in the brain imaging study responded to the scientific evidence of physiological damage from childhood abuse by recommending activities to help left–right hemisphere coordination, such as playing a musical instrument as well as psychotherapy. This, they thought, would help individuals integrate right-hemisphere emotions while maintaining left-hemisphere awareness, and so strengthen connections between the two hemispheres. Another neuro-imaging study has recently shown how the simple act of putting feelings into words actually calms the amygdala, a brain region involved in emotional processing, while other labelling and matching activities did not. In this study, functional magnetic resonance imaging (fMRI) showed that when the participants chose affect labels for images of faces exhibiting different emotions, activity increased in the brain's right ventrolateral prefrontal cortex region – an area associated with thinking in words about emotional experiences. By contrast, when they were involved in other exercises, the brain scans did not show these changes – indicating that only affect labelling, or putting emotions into words, makes a difference.[14]

These brain studies are informative, and often corroborative of traditional psychotherapeutic techniques which help calm and manage psychological suffering. However, they are of limited use when it comes to psychological healing, or transforming suffering into meaning. As is often said, 'the map is not the territory'. Jungian analyst Donald Kalsched offers a different perspective. He sees the barriers to psychological healing as archetypal in nature, rooted in the deep structures of the psyche. He suggests that they have a life-saving purpose, acting as defences of the personal spirit in what he calls an archetypal self-care system: when trauma strikes the developing child, a fragmentation of consciousness occurs in which the different parts of the psyche are organized by an archetypal pattern that protects the disintegration of the personality. Typically, the 'personal spirit' – the innocent, vulnerable inner core of the personality – goes into hiding, while another part of psyche grows up too fast and becomes precociously adapted to the outer world, often as a 'false self', which is like Diana's 'mask'. It then becomes the role of this false self to protect the vulnerable personal spirit at all costs. The cost may, however, be too high. What was initially created to save the personal spirit may become entrenched in the psyche and operate indiscriminately, going to any lengths to maintain the protective split by attacking anyone or anything that comes near it. In extreme cases it may even, through suicide, kill the host personality in which the personal spirit is housed This defensive structure often appears in dreams as a daimonic or terrifying figure, either protective or persecutory of the personal spirit, which typically appears as a vulnerable, young, often feminine, child or animal.[15]

Kalsched characterizes this archetypal self-care system as coming from the numinous, mythopoetic, archetypal layer of the psyche. In Diana's drawings, the 'snakewomen' may have arisen as an image of the personal spirit which was buried in the realm of the blood-soul, while the Hekatoncheires appeared as the image of the daimonic figure which defended the split. This split may have protected the young and vulnerable Diana when she was a child, but it had long since served its purpose and was now a danger to her psychological well-being. So the Hekatoncheires, the guardian of her buried emotions, affects and feelings, would first need to be worked with and depotentiated before the Olympians and Titans could once again be reunited.

Diana's personal story is her own. But it may also, through the workings of the collective unconscious in which all individuals are embedded, be part of a far wider Western 'cultural complex' which is now demanding attention. Originally it was none other than Mother Gaia, nature herself, who sent the Hekatoncheires to help overcome the Titans and stop the destruction of that ten-year war with the Olympians. Western consciousness may once have needed to bury the Titans, in order to protect a threatened disintegration of its developing culture. The resulting struggle between blood-soul and spirit-soul may have created the necessary tension for that culture's many achievements. But just as for individuals the once useful archetypal defences of the personal spirit can become stifling, so those defences may become damaging at cultural levels too. As Diana's personal story continues in the next chapter, it may offer wider lessons for a healing of the Olympian–Titan split – and for the role of the goddess Themis in their reconciliation.

Chapter 3

Themis calls the gods together

When shining Themis, flushed with beauty, drew with her golden horses towards the stairway to Olympus, the gods and goddesses rejoiced. Already they revered her, and with her marriage to Zeus, something seemed to be fulfilled. Some even say she was brought by the Fates, those three workwomen who between them spin, weave and cut the thread of every human life. Others, not so willing perhaps to admit that there is a power older and stronger than even Zeus, father of gods and men, remember it differently: the Fates, they say, were the daughters of this union, and most particularly honoured by their father. But what seems sure is that there was something fated about Themis's arrival among the golden thrones of Olympus – something as necessary and inescapable as the Fates themselves, and the great natural cycle of birth, flowering and death which they uphold.[1]

What did Themis bring to this marriage between Titans and Olympians? The root of her name is the verb *tithemi*, which means to place, to set and lay down, and also to fix and determine. So Themis brings the boundaries and right order set not by human rules or laws, but by that which underlies them – an archetypal order which is both natural and divine. This order had existed since the beginning of time: to some, Themis was known as Mother Earth by another name, so strongly does she carry Gaia's attributes. Thus Themis also forms a bridge to the new divine order, the new psychological ruling principle, from the very beginning of the old. This bridging function is a lasting one, right through Zeus's reign and beyond. In the first century CE, that tireless travel writer Pausanias found a shrine to Themis on his way to the very seat of patriarchal government, the acropolis of Athens; and inscriptions to Gaia-Themis – Earth and Right – have survived there to this day.[2] Themis's energy is still part of the psychological inheritance of Western individuals and societies. Importantly, her divine and natural law, her *themis*, has continued to operate through all the centuries of patriarchal organisation, and is still at work as Western consciousness seems to be struggling to move beyond it towards a new relationship of the qualities it knows as 'masculine' and 'feminine'.

Themis was not the only wife to share Zeus's couch, nor even, some say, the first: that place, they say, is held by Metis, another Titaness and mother of the goddess Athene. Themis was certainly not alone either in attracting Zeus's attention as he pursued and conquered, enticed and seduced, the myriad goddesses, nymphs and mortal women into whom he so abundantly scattered his seed. These matings, experienced here as terror, there as bliss, here as rape, there as ecstatic surrender, can be seen as the very image of the new patriarchal order's subjection and subsuming of the old, the sky-gods' conquest of the ancient deities of earth and nature. But the place of Themis in the new order is quite distinct. She was not pursued and raped, nor ecstatically impregnated and abandoned; she was not visited for a single moment of joy or outrage and left to marvel at the coming of the god. Themis was brought to Olympus by the Fates: psychologically, this marriage seems to tell of an inexorable development in Western consciousness.

There is one very particular image of Themis on Olympus, and of her marriage: she sits next to Zeus, leaning intimately towards him as they converse wisely together. This suggests a very different relationship with the god from that of the other goddess-wives. Themis was not swallowed up by Zeus, like the Titaness Metis, or locked with him in an everlastingly passionate love affair and power struggle, like Hera. And together with this uniquely cooperative relationship with the father of gods and men, Themis has a uniquely powerful role. Whenever there is need for the Olympians to come together in council, she is the one to summon them. When she 'ranges all about' and seeks them out, then they respond. These are images of cooperation between the old order and the new, not conquest. Psychologically, they suggest the possibility of partnership between Titan and Olympian, between the natural, instinctual law and differentiated consciousness, between the laws of the body and those of the mind, and between nature and culture. The images of Themis on Olympus suggest that through all the dominance of Western patriarchal consciousness, which has brought the honouring of mind over body, spirit over matter, intellect over instincts, there has been a psychological potential for a different way of being. It is also *themis*, as the old Greeks knew, that woman and men, 'feminine' and 'masculine' come together and unite in love.[3]

This psychological potential may be what Western consciousness is now groping towards. The children of Themis and Zeus, the outcome of this union of the old order with the new, suggest some of the rewards it may bring. The deities' three daughters are the Horai: Eunomia (Good Order), Eirene (Peace) and Dike (Just Retribution, or Justice – whose story is explored in Chapter 6). What better qualities for a new god, ambitious to establish his kingdom, to bring about! To today's rational consciousness, the story can seem no more than a transparent attempt to justify the annexation of the old order by the new. Yet these children of Zeus and Themis carry more than a culture-bound story of Olympian politics. Their collective name means 'the correct moment', in the sense of the one which is precisely right, and they are always truthful. They have a particular relationship to time's natural rhythms, for as well as being known as the Hours, they are also called the Seasons. They are constant in their attention to human activities: their special charge is to guard the gates of Olympus and roll away the heavy cloud that settles over it, so dispelling the fog that may obscure the gods from human hearts and minds.[4] So the qualities the Horai represent come at their due time into human consciousness, and are embedded in it as part of its own cycles. Their role as gatekeepers to the psychological energies of which the deities are images is a reminder that a truthful attention to 'the right moment' is what is needed to move beyond the clouds of unconsciousness to greater psychological awareness.

So Themis unites the gods in assemblies, and gives birth to the capacity to attend to the energies they represent in a way that is ordered, peaceful, and just. Psychologically, these qualities suggest that there is an inherent, archetypal energy which draws together the different psychological structures which the gods and goddesses represent. It seems to be an inner law that where there is a high degree of psychic differentiation – as imaged by the different gods on Olympus, each with their own attributes and responsibilities – then there is also a force that pulls these different elements towards unity. Jung called these complementary opposites Logos and Eros, and identified them with 'masculine' and 'feminine' energies. If one is not honoured more than the other, they can work together in a constant rhythm of separation and reunification: 'it is the function of Eros to unite what Logos has sundered'.[5] This rhythm suggests that when dis-harmony and even warfare among different elements of psyche lead to neurotic suffering, then there is also the potential, in *themis*, to bring these elements creatively together. As we shall see in this and succeeding chapters, this potential operates both at the level of the individual psyche and in groups and societies.

Importantly, this has nothing to do with perfect harmony. Themis brings the deities together, but they still squabble among themselves, fight for their own favourites and disagree about the best course of action. Nor does their coming together dull their individual qualities. Glorious, abundant Aphrodite still kindles joy in the world of the senses, and shrewd, grey-eyed Athene still brings her unique skill to the applications of human craft. Fleet-footed, elusive Hermes still delights in the tangle and traffic of the human marketplace, and cool, analytic Apollo still shoots his arrows of pure thought from afar. The process that Jung called 'individuation', becoming more fully the person one is meant to be, has to do with becoming not more perfect but more whole, more respectful of different psychological energies and more able to accept self-division and live with it creatively. As he said, 'one does not become enlightened by imagining figures of light, but by making the darkness conscious'.[6]

Diana's story continues

Meeting with her own psychological darkness and finding a way to reunite with her blood-soul, and her Titanic emotions, affects and instincts, became Diana's task. Themis's energy was exactly the one she needed to draw together, in awareness and appreciation, the different voices and aspects of the psyche. And it was with those mighty Hekatoncheires, with whom we left her at the end of the last chapter, that she began to find it.

Diana was not able to talk about that picture (Figure 2.4) as a whole; it was too overwhelming for her. Her rational, analytic consciousness did not have words for the long-repressed Titans and their terrifying oppressor. But she could begin to identify individual figures in the picture's seemingly undifferentiated mass of heads and bodies, and to speak of the feelings and emotions attached to them. It was almost as if the pieces of her blood-soul had to be recollected one by one. Many of the figures in that image led to memories of her childhood, and painful and terrifying experiences with her mother and grandfather. But others brought memories of happier times which had also been swept into the underworld of affect. Just as Themis brought the gods together, Diana was able to start bringing together these different psychological contents. The analysis became the container within which her repressed Titanic feelings were 'summoned to council' and reunited with images and memories from her childhood.

As each image was remembered, experienced and heard, and then held in consciousness with all the others, a shift in Diana's psyche began. The Hekatoncheires were no longer needed to keep their guard on the Titanic world of her emotions. Once her blood-soul was heard and experienced, her intense emotions and the images themselves began to change and become less fearful. The process of 'coming to council' and giving voice to all present helped to produce that 'right moment' where psychological change could happen. Over the next several months, the pictures that Diana produced began to alter. Figure 3.1 is representative of the development that took place.

This picture shows a marked development from Figure 2.4. Now, instead of an undifferentiated mass of heads, bodies and limbs, a more complete figure has emerged, which includes a head and a body as well. Mind and body, spirit-soul and blood-soul are beginning to be reunited. In this picture, the main figure's expression shows a deep sadness, and the protective crossing of the arms and legs suggest that Diana's emerging self is becoming more bounded and able to protect itself. There are also fewer images in the picture, which indicates that there has been a healing of some of the psychic splits, and the expressions on many of the faces are either neutral or positive. More of the faces and figures are female, too, which suggests that different aspects of the feminine are coming into consciousness to create in Diana a greater sense of her own feminine being. But hiding in the middle is a frightening masculine face with open mouth, a figure that Diana identified as her grandfather.

Figure 3.1 Diana's emerging self.

Perhaps this is also an image of the Titan Kronos in his negative aspect, as the one who eats his own children, and a representation of the archetypal force which drove her grandfather to devour Diana for his own selfish desires. Even though he had died years before, what he represented is still a part of Diana's psyche, threatening to destroy her new feminine development. Yet the feminine aspects of her psyche are also growing around him, which brings hope that these will, in time, emerge as the centre of her own being.

Diana then had a powerful dream. As Jung says, in sleep we can become acquainted with the reaction of the serpent, that deeply instinctual part of ourselves. And as we will see in Chapter 5, dreams are also the realm of Themis, who ruled at Delphi with the serpent Python as the oracular voice of the earth. So once those mighty Hekatoncheires had been depotentiated, the energy of the goddess could now lead Diana to a new experience of the feminine and of herself. She dreamed:

> I'm running on a path through the woods. It's dusk or dawn, and it's fall. The leaves are beautiful on the trees. Some people wanted to come with me, but I said no. I felt like a long distance runner. The woods were dark, really dark, but I feel wonderful, really exhilarated.

In recounting this dream, Diana said that this was the first time she had ever felt like a single person, without all the different aspects that her pictures had shown. During sleep, while her accustomed consciousness was quieted, the serpent and oracular voice had spoken, and given her an experience of wholeness that was transformative. In the dream, she has found a new path, and it is a path through nature. This grounding in nature has given her the strength to say no to the 'people' who want to come with her. She experiences a new sense of determination and perseverance, feeling the energy to become a 'long distance runner'. Even though the darkness is still all around her, and Diana is not yet 'out of the woods', she feels wonderful, really exhilarated – emotions which are in striking contrast to her earlier feelings of disgust and self-hate. Once again, her psyche and her conscious understanding had come together in the 'right moment' which enabled her old, false sense of self to give way to a new grounding in her unique feminine being.

The impact of this powerful dream was reflected in a new drawing, this time a self-portrait (Figure 3.2). The development from the undifferentiated mass of heads and bodies to the emergence of different feminine figures has continued dramatically: now for the first time there is an image of Diana alone, as a single being. She said that it showed her feeling strong and grounded, which was something she had never experienced in quite this way before.

In Diana's self-portrait, there seems to be a sense of peace and power in her eyes, which look directly at the viewer from a youthful face that also evokes the feminine wisdom of the ages. The detail on the face strikingly and accurately reflects the anatomical configuration of the muscles underlying the skin: it seems that Diana is becoming embodied. At the same time, her neck-lace draws attention to the place where 'body' meets 'head', the throat area which the ancient Indian system of the subtle body sees as the seat of the fifth chakra or energy centre, the place of purification. At the centre of the

Figure 3.2 Diana alone.

necklace there is a diamond, which brings images of constancy and harmony, light and purity. Western psychological interpretations have suggested that the fifth chakra has to do with the coming of psychological awareness, with an understanding of the relationship between the inner world and perceptions of the one 'outside', and with a cleansing of the voice from the false speech that can come from the persona or social mask.[7] Diana seems to be finding her own 'true' voice, which can now express her new sense of herself.

She has also drawn herself with long, wavy hair surrounding her face. Symbolically, hair can represent the life force, as well as the thoughts that come from the head. So it seems that Diana's energy is becoming stronger, and there is a powerful connection with the head, or mind. The frightening figures of earlier pictures have not completely disappeared: they can still be seen, entangled among those flowing locks. But now they are becoming more integrated: they are now no longer independent threats, as her grandfather was when she was small, but inner figures which can be understood as manageable by her own power of thought.

As *themis* energy continued its work of calling together the many parts that split when she was a child, Diana was able to make repair in the outer world as well as the inner: she could now meet her chaotic mother, without feeling her own psyche fracturing and creating hallucinations as it had so terrifyingly done in the past. Then came another picture (Figure 3.3).

This picture shows Diana's deepening appreciation of herself as a woman, a strikingly different image of the feminine from the overwhelming negative one represented by her mother, which she had so determinedly rejected. That rejection had been achieved at great cost – a loss of her feminine self. Now however she has found a connection to her breasts, an image of her own mothering and nurturing self. She is finally connected to a more grounded and powerful feminine energy. Diana entitled this picture 'Strong'.

The imagery of this reconnection with the feminine, as it emerged first through Diana's 'snakewomen' and then through progressively complete figures of her womanly self, brings echoes of another powerful serpent goddess. This Minoan goddess, whose power was vibrantly alive in Crete about 1600 BCE (Figure 3.4), is less than 12 inches tall, but her energy is enormous as she proudly displays her breasts for all to see. The snakes she brandishes in each hand, it has been suggested, may be the snakes of life and death, manifestations of the ancient capacity of the goddess to give and withdraw life. This power has long been revered and feared. It is 'in her blood' as much as her 'blood mysteries' of menstruation and birth, and legend tells too of attempts by masculine forces to claim it as their own. The Medusa, for instance, became known as a terrifyingly paralysed and paralysing feminine force; only her snaky hair remained as a reminder of her once-great origins by the time her story was told. Yet when the hero Perseus killed her, he drew from the veins of her right arm and her left two vials of blood which still carried the ancient power of life and death. Some say the goddess Athene would have given both to the healer Aesclepius, had not Hades, lord of the underworld, protested at this threatened loss of souls for his kingdom. The final fate of those vials is not known: we can at least imagine that they have been passed on through the generations, so that it is forever in the blood-soul of every human being to work in their own way for life or death.[8]

In the Minoan image, that power was still with the goddess. The small lion that sits on her head is a reminder that this energy – at once protective and

Figure 3.3 Diana feels her feminine strength.

destructive, warlike and maternal – had been hers from Neolithic times right into the Christian era. Some eight thousand years ago, in Old Europe, the goddess is imaged as giving birth between two guardian lions or lionesses. In the Bronze Age ancient Near East, the great goddess Ishtar-Innana is flanked

Figure 3.4 The Snake goddess reappears. Herakleion Archaeological Museum, Crete, Hellenic Ministry of Culture – Archaeological Receipts Fund.

by the creatures, and in her war-like aspect hymned as roaring with their voice. The goddess Cybele, now the Great Mother, journeys to Rome in a chariot drawn by lions, and as late as the fifteenth century they are seen again as guardians, now of Mary, the Mother of God. But the lion carries 'masculine' as well as 'feminine' energy. It is the principle of fire, associated with the sun; it represents majesty, virility and deathless courage. The small lion that appears on the Minoan goddess's head may be a cub, suggesting that a young consciousness was emerging around 1600 BCE which could have grown to include masculine and feminine energies in a balanced dynamic. There is even a connection, through the Hebrew word *iblia*, which means both 'lion' and 'heart', with the 'blood-centre', or 'soul', represented by the tribe of Judah. In the development of Western consciousness, however, the lion became associated with the god-realm, the mortal enemy of the serpent and, among many others, a symbol for Christ.[9]

Conscious developments, however, do not mean that unconscious energies are lost. When Diana made conscious connection with this wealth of imagery in its feminine form, she could feel a new strength. Now she could begin to address her very negative relationship with the masculine. Once again, from that oracular source, she received a dream:

> I'm in my grandmother's old house, and I confront my grandfather. I'm beating him up, and telling him that he molested me. I keep flashing back to being a kid, and how he'd grab me, then I'd become an adult in the dream and hit him.
>
> I wasn't scared of my grandfather at all. I'm totally unafraid. I think I'm going to rape him with the biggest item I can find.
>
> Then I'm in a scene in a theatre where *The Wizard of Oz* is playing. I had to call someone to let them know about what was playing. A woman beside me gives me the change I need to make the call. She reminds me of my grandmother.

Diana is now in the grandmother's – or 'Great Mother's – house, the realm of the archetypal feminine to which Gaia, Themis and Rhea belong. With her new grounding in the feminine, she has found her strength and her voice, and can confront the devouring destructive masculine, imaged as her grandfather. As she flips between being the vulnerable child and a powerful woman, Diana connects with her traumatized past in a new way. The split that Donald Kalsched described, between the vulnerable personal spirit and the tyrannical persecutory figure of the archetypal self-care system, is finally beginning to heal.[10] Diana's new-found power needs taming: understandably, she has a moment of inflated identification with the tyrannical 'Great Father', and wants to 'rape' in her turn, as violently as she can. But before this might happen, the scene changes, and so does her perception. When she described the scene with *The Wizard of Oz*, Diana said she was reminded of the wicked witch who melted, and the frightening wizard who turned out to be a pathetic figure. With this new understanding, she was able to disengage from these traumatizing aspects in her psyche, and their fragmenting and tormenting effects on her began to lessen.

In this new situation, Diana wants to reach out and tell what she has seen. A woman beside her gives her the 'change' she needs – which is the new connection with the ancient feminine, the energy of 'the grandmother'. Diana can now relate to the destructive masculine in a more constructive way. She does not kill it, or rape it in revenge, but, as her next picture (Figure 3.5) shows, she is able to restrain it.

In this picture, the Ouranos/Kronos energy in Diana's psyche has been

Figure 3.5 Diana restrains the destructive masculine.

chained and restricted, and she has assimilated some of its power as a neces-sary step in her continuing journey towards forming a more positive relation-ship with the masculine. There may be cultural parallels here, as the evolving feminism of the past decades has sought both to restrain the ways of patri-archal Western culture and to incorporate some of its power. This is not the end of the story, as it was not for Diana, because it denies all the positive dynamism of relationship between masculine and feminine energies. But as it was a necessary step for her, so it may have been for the evolution of the culture. Towards the end of her analysis, Diana produced a drawing which marked the culmination of two years' analytical work (Figure 3.6).

This is a mandala, a Sanskrit word for 'circle', which describes the circles drawn in religious rituals. From Native American and Tibetan sand paintings to Gothic rose windows and Hindu *yantras*, the symbolism of mandalas has fostered meditation, protection and healing of individuals and cultures across both time and space. When a mandala appears spontaneously in the course of psychological work, as it did for Diana, it often signals a new psychic arrangement, a reordering of the personality. It is an image of wholeness. In the work of individuation, the endless work of becoming more of oneself, this image of wholeness can both protect the fragmented and fearful conscious

Figure 3.6 Diana's image of wholeness.

mind and help bring it into greater balance with the unconscious. Very often, as Jung discovered for himself, the creation of mandalas can seem literally lifesaving. When he was plunged into the extreme psychological experiences that threatened to overwhelm him after his life-defining break with Freud, he found himself making mandala after mandala, until he lost count of how many there were. Significantly, once he had the dream which he felt brought him to 'the centre' that for him was the goal of psyche's journey of individuation, and to the idea of the Self as 'the principle and archetype of orientation and meaning', he no longer felt a need to make mandalas at all. The symbol had done its creative psychic work and brought him to a new stage of consciousness.[11] The basic motif of mandalas, Jung thought:

> is the premonition of a centre of personality, a kind of central point within the psyche, to which everything is related, by which everything is arranged, and which is itself a source of energy. The energy of the central point is manifested in the almost irresistible compulsion and urge *to become what one is*, just as every organism is driven to assume the form that is characteristic of its nature, no matter what the circumstances. This centre is not felt or thought of as the ego but, if one may so express it, as the *self*.[12]

Jung's idea of the Self[13] could hardly have been more important to his own experience or to the theoretical work that grew out of it. His insight into the existence of an archetype which is both the circumference and the centre of psychic totality and which orders psychic contents to bring a sense of meaning, brought with it a first inkling of his 'personal myth'; without this, he said at the end of his long life, he might have lost his orientation altogether and been obliged to abandon his psychological research. For him, the Self was a reality – 'not a doctrine or theory, but an image born of nature's own workings'. Yet he was also aware of the impossibility of 'proving' with the conscious mind a concept that embraces the whole of psyche, both conscious and unconscious. He had never yet, he told one enquirer, found the stable and definite centre to the unconscious that the Self represented and he did not 'believe' such a centre existed. What he did believe, however, was that 'the thing I call the self is a dream of totality'. This is no dismissal. For Jung, dreams are a vital constituent of psychic reality, 'the best possible representation at the moment for a fact as yet unknown'.[14] Human experience bears this out. 'To have a dream', whether by night or by day and as the unfolding of countless social revolutions as well as individual lives can attest, is to have an intimation of a psychological possibility as yet unrealized but nevertheless potentially available, because already imagined.

Dreams, like other conduits from the unconscious, carry their messages through images that become emotions and stories; it is through such accumulations that consciousness can connect with the Self's deep and continuing work. Jung's own imagery for the Self drew most often on the Christian tradition: for him, the archetype was exemplified by the huge wealth of the symbolism of Christ. Yet Jung was also aware of the universality of the Self's manifestations in the world's great religions. This in itself was, for him, a sure indication of its reality: 'The self is a living person and has always been there.'[15]

And that, in a very different way, Diana's experience would also reveal. The striking similarities between the imagery and stories of Themis and the concept of the Self offer corroboration for the concept from a time and place in which Jung had not thought to seek. Just as the goddess brings together disparate psychological contents into her own 'right order', so the Self, as both circumference and centre of psyche, brings the personality to the greatest possible unity and wholeness. Just as *themis* energy stems from nature itself, so the Self has its roots in the body 'indeed in the body's chemical elements': without this essential link with the world of instinct, says Jung, there can be no Self at all.[16] Both the goddess and the Self thus offer images and intimations of a deeper, perhaps more instinctual, psychic ordering, which goes beyond any that the 'Olympian' ego alone can achieve.

So it was for Diana. In the mandala which is her own image of the work of the Self, the snake/serpent that appeared in her very first picture of the shattered feminine has returned. But now it contains the image of wholeness rather than being entwined with elements of her psyche. It has become the guardian of her psychological state and process, distinct from her image of herself rather than merged with it; she is now connected with the deep serpent wisdom in her psyche, not tormented by it. Within the serpent's containing circumference, 12 lion heads have formed to create an inner circle. The lion, now fully grown, appears once again with the snake energy, bringing to a new stage of development the relationship of beast and serpent that was prefigured in the image of the Cretan snake goddess.

The mandala brings yet more. At its centre there is an eight-pointed star, which contains another, this time with four points. A star signals the presence of a divinity, supremacy, the eternal, and the undying. It symbolizes the highest attainment, hope, and the eyes of the night. The eight-pointed star is especially connected with Ishtar, the Queen of Heaven, who herself, as we have seen, is intimately related to the lion. It is also a symbol of the goddess Venus, whose planet is the most brilliant at the end of the old day and the dawn of the new, and who presides over motherhood and the unions of both physical and spiritual love. This profoundly feminine symbol can also be said to have a masculine counterpart: the eight-pointed star has also to do with the regenerative power of the rising sun. The eight and four points of the star have further significance too. Jung posited that numbers, far from being invented by human ingenuity, might just as well have been discovered as pre-existing representations of archetypal patterns; in this understanding, they are endowed with qualities that have still to be brought to conscious awareness.

Through the study of cultural anthropology, comparative religions, dreams and images, Jung found that four is generally seen as a feminine number, associated with wholeness. Eight is a double quaternity and, as an individuation symbol in mandalas, plays almost as great a role as the quaternity itself.[17] Here again, the four- and eight-pointed star can be seen to symbolize many aspects of *themis* energy – the energy of a feminine divinity which guides towards wholeness as the star guides through the darkness of night.

When Diana brought the mandala image to analysis, it created a resonance in the session in a way that no words could possibly express, and a psychic connection far beyond the everyday world of ego consciousness. The analysis had come full circle, and the mandala provided an image of what had been accomplished. Diana had reached a new state of integration and relationship to the unconscious, a relationship that included powerful archetypal images of the ancient feminine. She had known nothing of Themis or of her sister serpent goddess, and neither had Pamela. Yet the images had emerged spontaneously from Diana's psyche, from the mysterious and powerful world of the unconscious which contains the archetypes whose myriad images have appeared to human beings throughout the ages.

The symbols of wholeness appearing in Diana's mandala were powerful images of the healing that had occurred in her psyche. This would be significant enough. But some two years after her therapy had ended, while Pamela was researching Themis and what she represented, she came for the first time across an image of the goddess that added yet another dimension to Diana's story (Figure 3.7).

In this illustration of Themis as the oracle of Delphi, taken from a vase that dates from the fifth century BCE, Themis's emblem is shown as an eight-pointed star inside two circles, the same image that Diana had drawn as the centre of her mandala. This discovery seemed to confirm that the goddess's energy had indeed been guiding Diana's analytic process throughout, entirely independently of the conscious awareness of either herself or Pamela.

After the mandala appeared, Diana graduated from school on time without postponement, and received her Masters degree. The hallucinations stopped when she developed an inner life, a relationship to the Titanic emotions and instincts, and to her own psychic process. Blood-soul and spirit-soul had been reunited once again.

Diana's unique story of the way in which those souls became severed can also illuminate the story of a whole culture. Western consciousness developed as it did. Its creation myths have taken us from the splitting of Ouranos from Gaia, through the tyrannical father gods who consume their children, to the Olympians who buried the Titans, and the era of a patriarchal God in which the snake was demonized and the once harmonious relationship of humankind and nature destroyed. Western culture is still left with this mythological and psychological legacy. Yet there are other creation myths, even within the

Figure 3.7 Themis as the oracle of Delphi: 5th century BCE vase painting. Bildarchiv Preussischer Kulturbesitz/Art Resource, NY.

Western tradition. Although they have been largely forgotten, they still form part of the collective unconscious that underpins today's understandings, and are still available to offer their different energy for the future.

In the beginning, Eurynome, the Goddess of All Things,
rose naked from Chaos.
When she found there was nothing to stand on, she divided
the sea from the sky, and danced alone over the waves.
As she moved southwards, a wind sprang up behind her.
She made something which was of but not herself
with which to begin
a work of creation.

Eurynome wheeled about.
She caught hold of this north wind
rubbed and rubbed it between her hands and –
the great serpent Ophion appeared!
The Goddess danced and wildly danced, until
the Serpent coiled about those divine limbs and joined her.
Eurynome became pregnant.
Now she took the form of a dove, brooding on the waves until
she laid the Universal Egg.
She commanded Orphion to coil seven times about the egg, and wait.
He waited.
Then the egg began to move. The shell began to crack.
The egg split in two!
And from it emerged all that exists,
all that can be imagined,
all of them the children of Eurynome.
Above, the sun and moon and planets and stars.
Below, the earth with its mountains and rivers, its trees and plants.
And on the earth all the living creatures.[18]

How different might our culture now be if it had always remembered this pre-Hellenic Pelasgian myth, which dates from the fourth millennium BCE? The mythic images speak of a gentler way, a dance of creation that is connected to the instincts and the primal energies of the snake. Goddess and snake are once again united, and they take us back to the realm of Themis and the psychological energy she represents. This is the energy that healed Diana's deeply wounded feminine nature and helped her on her journey to reunite her blood-soul with her spirit-soul. Over the centuries, the language of the blood-soul has been lost to collective consciousness. But it is not forgotten, and now it is beginning to be reclaimed, as the next chapter explores.

Chapter 4

The language of the blood-soul

The split between Diana's analytic mind and suffering emotions was uniquely her own. But it also reflected the split between the spirit-soul and the blood-soul which for many centuries has been a hallmark of Western societies. In this split, and with the repression of the blood-soul, much of the ability to understand the language of the body and the information it communicates has been lost. And as we have seen, this has brought a whole variety of bodily symptoms and psychological dis-eases that seem so characteristic of the times.

But now, some of the language of the blood-soul is being recovered and becoming more intelligible. Through new medical technology, Apollonian reason is serving to make the deep language of human nature more conscious. Spirit-soul is beginning to meet with blood-soul as it discovers that the body as well as the mind has its intelligence. Current research is only beginning to decode this intelligence and its laws. But it is documenting scientifically what may have been known for centuries only through intuition, poetic imagination or 'gut feeling': that there are systems in the body which communicate important information which needs to be understood for continuing health and growth. Research in emotional physiology and heart–brain interactions is sketching a more complete understanding not just of the way the heart-soul and the spirit-soul interact in individuals, but of ways in which they may operate between people as well.[1]

Scientific research has shown that the organs of the body, such as the heart, stomach, lungs, kidneys, and intestines are regulated by the autonomic nervous system, and that near each of them is a cluster of neurons which regulates the organ it serves. Each of these, in a way, operates as an information encoding and processing centre. Science, since it tends to see things through the lens of the mind, is now referring to these centres as 'little brains' within the body. Research in neurocardiology has established that the heart is one of the more powerful sensory organs – an information encoding and processing centre with an extensive intrinsic nervous system sophisticated enough to be seen as a 'heart brain'.[2] When this 'heart brain' is viewed from the perspective of the body, it seems to correspond perfectly with the ancient experience of *thymos*, the blood- or heart-soul. This processing centre of the heart enables it to learn, remember, and make functional decisions independently of the brain's cerebral cortex. So sentiments like 'I'll hold you in my heart' may be much more than just metaphorically true.

Research has also shown that the heart has clear rhythmic patterns when different emotions are experienced. Figure 4.1 gives an image of this, created through the monitoring of the heart beat with an electrocardiogram (ECG) and calculation of heart-rate variability, or heart rhythms, during different emotional experiences.[3]

As Figure 4.1 shows, during the experience of negative emotions such as frustration, anger or anxiety, heart rhythms become more erratic and disordered. When people experience the 'positive' emotions, like interest, appreciation, love, joy or compassion, the heart rhythms shift into a highly ordered or *coherent* pattern. 'Coherence', in physics, has a particular meaning: it describes the ordered or constructive distribution of power within a wave form. But individuals have a sense of psychological 'coherence' too: when they are in a positive emotional state, they are likely also to feel 'together' or 'good in their skin'. This sense can be seen as the working of *themis* energy, as it brings together the different psychological contents with the blood-soul. People also know the sense of psychological 'disorder', even 'dissociation' of psychic contents that comes with negative emotions, and when *themis* energy is not operating freely. We all have experience of the possibly 'erratic' behaviour that can result when we are taken over by one of those clusters of psychic energy that Jung called complexes, or 'splinter psyches'. These clusters of energy operate independently of our will and conscious ego: 'We don't have complexes', as Jung once said, 'they have us.' Although no heart-wave studies have been done on individuals overwhelmed by a complex, a study on people with multiple personality disorder may shed light on what actually happens in the body during a 'complex attack'. This study showed that each 'personality' had its own distinctive and recognizable heart pattern, which suggests that similarly distinctive patterns are likely to exist

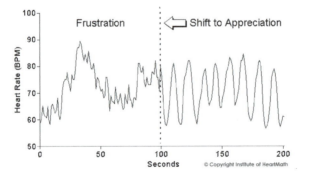

Figure 4.1 Emotions reflected in heart rhythm patterns. Courtesy Institute of HeartMath Research Center.

within any individual as they experience different mood states, or the different 'feeling tones' of different complexes.[4]

The research into the relationship between heart waves and emotions suggests just how literally 'heart-felt' these positive and negative psychological feelings may be. At some level, it seems the 'mind–body' split, with which consciousness is so familiar, may not exist at all. It is when an individual cannot understand the language of the blood-soul well enough to appreciate the negative emotions produced by the body and the information which it is trying to communicate that a psychological split is created, sometimes so deep that separate personalities come into being. But if appreciation, love, joy, or compassion is turned towards the split, complex, or 'personality', *themis* energy may bring the parts together into a more coherent whole.

The research also suggests that the heart is an emotionally intelligent communicator, capable of sending information throughout the body's systems. Experiments have shown that the signals the heart sends to the brain via the nervous system influence cognitive perception, cognition, and emotional processing. Many of these processes operate at a much higher speed than thoughts, and frequently bypass the mind's linear reasoning process entirely. This too may help to explain the experience of being 'taken over' by a psychological complex. In that experience, the conscious mind has no control over what happens, and we may not even recognize that part of ourselves which is temporarily in psychological charge. 'But I *never* do something like that!' we may say, when we realize that we have just done precisely that thing. Then, when the brain and mind catch up with the information they have received from the heart, it becomes possible to try to work out what happened and what to do about it.

The heart's communications do not reach only the brain and mind. Research has also shown that information travels throughout the body through electromagnetic field interactions. The heart generates the body's most powerful and most extensive rhythmic electromagnetic field: compared to the field produced by the brain, the electrical component of the heart's field is about 60 times greater in amplitude, and approximately 5000 times stronger. This heart field permeates every cell in the body. So whether the heart is communicating distress or appreciation, that message is being felt throughout the system at its very deepest levels. When the emotional experience is positive and the heart field is coherent, then other bodily systems also become involved: two or more of the body's oscillatory systems, such as respiration, blood pressure, rhythms in the digestive system and brain waves, become *entrained* or *synchronized* and oscillate at the same frequency. This helps the mind and body to come into *resonance*, when there is increased synchronization between the sympathetic and parasympathetic branches of the autonomous nervous system, and entrainment between the heart rhythms, oscillatory systems and alpha rhythms in the brain. The description of mind–body *resonance* sounds much like Jung's understanding of the importance of connection with the serpent wisdom, cited in Chapter 2, and his assertion that if consciousness and the instinctual centres are not in practically the same tune or rhythm, 'under particularly unfavourable conditions one can be killed'.[5]

Importantly, conscious achievement of this deep mind–body rhythm seems to be an inherent part of human ability; *themis* energy is available to us all. Figure 4.2 shows this process at work among 30 people, with images of the brain showing as a mean topographical map, and the lighter shading showing when the heart rhythms and the brain's alpha waves have become synchronized. The brain image on the left shows the percentage of alpha activity in different regions of the brain that was synchronized to the heartbeat when the participants were in a normal resting condition. They were then asked to move into feeling deep appreciation for someone or something that they loved. The image on the right shows that once this state of appreciation was achieved and the heart rhythm moved into a coherent mode, substantially more of the alpha activity in brain became synchronized to the heart and shifted from the right frontal area to the left hemisphere and radiated outward. These observations may be related to findings indicating that increased left hemisphere activity is associated with happiness and euphoria while increased right hemisphere activity is associated with depression and negative affect.[6] However, this experiment also gives another image of mind–body synchronization, and the state of *resonance*, and shows how this can be fostered when the conscious mind is turned towards positive thoughts and feelings.

How might the state of resonance be experienced outside the laboratory and in everyday life? At the beginning of Diana's analysis, the discordance of rhythms between her body and her mind can be imagined: the Hekatoncheires gave an image of the level of her distress and the lack of coherent communication between the two. Once she was able to gain an interest in and appreciation for the communications from her unconscious and messages from her blood-soul, however, her images and her relationship to them began to shift. A coherent wave pattern was developing, it can be imagined, between heart and mind, synchronizing the two. Then the healing process could begin.

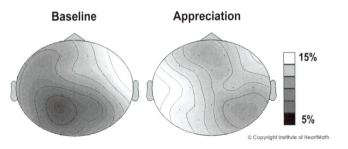

Figure 4.2 Alpha activity synchronized to the cardiac cycle. Courtesy Institute of HeartMath Research Center.

Diana was able to experience the emergence of *coherence* in her sense of self, rooted in the rhythms of her being. Her bodily and mental systems became more *resonant*. In this state, people feel more 'in the flow' as body, emotions and mind seemed to be working together to produce a feeling of well-being; intuitive abilities are heightened, and there may be synchronicities – those meaningful coincidences that come from a felt sense of 'fit' between inner and outer worlds. For Diana, there was *resonance* in her dream about running alone on the path in the woods, feeling wonderfully exhilarated. This experience was also pictured in her final mandala, which showed a state of inner harmony and balance, and imaged a new connection with the snake energies which represented her blood-soul.

In psycho-physiological resonance, then, there is an experience of balance between the blood-soul and spirit-soul, and the beginning of healing the mind–body split. This coming together of the two souls and sense of harmony between inner and outer worlds brings many benefits. Studies have shown that anxiety, depression, panic disorder, and post-traumatic stress disorder have all been improved. Blood pressure has been reduced, as has the need for medication for patients with cardiac arrhythmias, chronic fatigue, environmental sensitivity, fibromyalgia, and chronic pain. Physiologically, the antibody which is the body's first line of defence has been shown to increase. In one experiment, healthy and cancerous human cells were both exposed to the same coherent ECG signal: the growth of the healthy cells was facilitated by 20 per cent, while the growth of the tumour cells was inhibited by the same amount.[7] So the deep harmonious rhythms of body and mind can also promote healing, from the physiological, to the emotional, to the psychological realm.

Fortunate people initially learn physiological coherence from their early caregivers. Attunement with their mother soothes negative affects and experiences and helps the child return to a sense of internal balance. Feelings of appreciation, love, and compassion help to create a powerful body memory within the developing child. This sense may also become associated with the developing ego itself, creating feelings of self-worth, and healthy self-love. But often this does not happen. When a culture values thinking over feeling, rationality over the irrational, and treats the body as 'machine', and its messages as 'problems', this imbalance will tend to create non-coherent individual systems which perpetuate the mind–body split. Importantly, though, these systems are not fixed. A more positive experience of love and appreciation for the messages of the blood-soul can help produce coherent patterns, and as these become ever more familiar to the body and the brain, they will be established in the neural architecture as a new, stable baseline or norm. This norm will then serve as a set point or frame of reference that the system strives to maintain. In psychological language, a new attitude has been created, which will enable positive emotions and coherent physiological patterns progressively to replace maladaptive emotional patterns and stressful responses, and so create a new way of being. Blood-soul and spirit-soul will once more be in dialogue, and *themis* energy will be restored.

This is important for individual well-being, and relationships *within* the individual. But it seems that it may have extraordinary implications for relationships *between* people as well. Research has shown that the powerful electromagnetic field generated by the heart can also, with sensitive magnetometers, be detected several feet away from the body. This field may also be 'felt' in another individual, so that affects like frustration, distress, fear, anger, and joy may actually be communicated from one person to another.[8] Many people have an intuitive sense that another doesn't 'feel right', that there is a misfit between the persona or 'mask' and what is going on inside. Now it seems that this sense has sound physiological roots: people who are sensitive to the electromagnetic field between themselves and others will often be able to 'feel' it.

More than this: it seems that the state of one person really can influence that of another at a very deep level. If someone maintains a coherent heart field through positive states of appreciation, love, joy or compassion, this can actually synchronize or entrain the heart field of the other. In Figure 4.3, two women sitting four feet apart were consciously feeling appreciation for each other. Their heart rhythms became synchronized – and the two hearts literally began beating as one. Figure 4.4 underlines the point: it shows how the heartbeats of a sleeping couple in a loving relationship became synchronized during sleep.[9]

Both these examples can be seen as powerful illustrations of *themis* energy at work. They are images of the way in which this energy gathers together to create a resonant whole which is the goddess's 'right order'. By contrast,

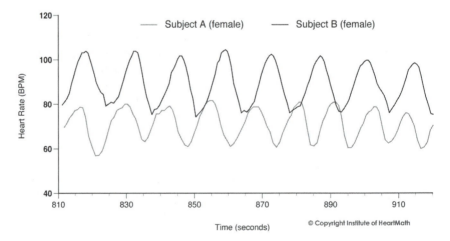

Figure 4.3 Heart rhythm entrainment between two people. Courtesy Institute of HeartMath Research Center.

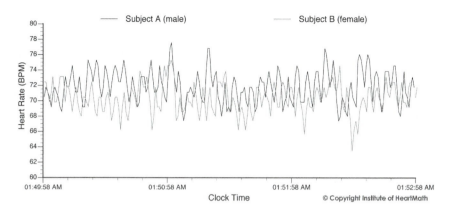

Figure 4.4 Heart rhythm entrainment between husband and wife during sleep. Courtesy Institute of HeartMath Research Center.

where *themis* energy is weak, the opposite may happen: a high level of discordant heart waves between married couples while they were interacting, for instance, has actually been shown to be a valid predictor of the probability of divorce.[10] So continued dissonance between two systems can drive them apart. This is probably as true within an individual mind-body system as it is between people.

To some ancient understandings, what is true of relationships within individuals and between them may also be true of the entire universe of which they are an inseparable part. Richard Wilhelm, the Sinologist and translator of the *I Ching*, recounts a story, supposedly from his own experience, that speaks to this awesome perspective. In today's language of the blood-soul, the story tells how a lack of mind–body coherence can not only affect human relationships, but also throw the very cosmic order into dissonance.

There was a terrible drought in a village in China. For months, and despite the most powerful prayers and rituals that the people could call on, there had not been a drop of rain. Finally, in desperation, the people decided to fetch the rainmaker. From another province, this very old, dried up man appeared. To the bewilderment of the people, he evoked no powers and demanded no rituals. Instead, he asked only for a quiet, small house, and locked himself away for three days. On the fourth day, the clouds gathered, and there was a great snowstorm – and this, at a time of year when there should have been no snow at all. Everyone was quite amazed, the village was alive with rumours about the old rainmaker and his powers.

'How did you do it?' asked Wilhelm.

'I didn't. I am not responsible', said the rainmaker.

'But what have you done these three days?'

'Oh, I can explain that. Where I come from, things are in order. Here they are out of order, they are not as they should be by the ordinance of heaven. So the whole country is out of Tao, and I am not in the natural order of things either, because I am in a disordered country. So I had to wait for three days until I was back in Tao. And then naturally the rain came.'[11]

Modern understanding may shy from the awesome implications of this concept of the vital interrelationship between individual and cosmos, and the responsibilities it places on each person to maintain their own inner harmony. What does seem likely, however, is that each of us communicates coherence or its opposite to those with whom we come into contact, at a level that goes beyond that of the conscious mind. In research with pairs of people who did not know the reason for the test, the ECG of the first person was detected in the electroencephalogram (EEG) and the alpha waves of the second, as well as on the second person's forearms. These findings suggest that our nervous systems act as antennae, which are tuned to and respond to the magnetic fields produced by the hearts of other individuals.[12]

This may also be the mechanism that underlies the phenomenon of transference and countertransference within the therapeutic process. In the work with Diana, and with many other analysands, it is often the resonant experience of *themis* energy that can create the basis for psychological change. This was something that Pamela also powerfully discovered in her work with John, who had been diagnosed as having paranoid schizophrenia.

John's ability to trust had been damaged early, from living with an abandoning and violent father and a deeply depressed mother who found it impossible to be present for her five children. By the time John was in his mid-twenties, he lived in a group home and attended therapy sporadically. It seemed almost impossible for him to sit in a room with another person for any extended period of time. As the weeks went by, his time in the consulting room increased little by little, but with it came the rage and violence that had initially been inflicted on him. I felt tested, battered emotionally with unrealistic demands and expectations, as if being asked whether I was strong enough to be able to be there for him.

In one pivotal session, John entered in a fury. I had disappointed him again, in yet another deal-breaking way. But this time, something different happened. His words left him, and he stared at me with the purest hate that I had ever experienced. I looked back, staying as open and present as I could manage. Suddenly, I began to feel a vice gripping round my heart which tightened and squeezed it to the point of pain. The thought came into my mind, 'This could actually kill me.' But I held on and kept John's gaze. Then the field broke and the hate left the room. His body relaxed and his eyes softened, which I had never seen in him before.

From that day on, he was different. He never missed a session, and came with questions, experiences, and a lovely openness. As he learned to trust me, he was also learning to trust himself, his own feelings, and instincts. He eventually moved out of the group home, got his own apartment, friends, and a job. John was well on his way to living a new and satisfying heartfelt existence.

What had happened? In the pivotal session, a breakthrough had occurred. John had learned from years of abuse and abandonment that his fragile heart-soul needed protection. No one was allowed to come near, and his paranoia had served that purpose well. In Kalsched's trauma model, explored in Chapter 2, John's personal spirit had been vehemently guarded by an archetypal self-care system that would rather kill or be killed than expose the vulnerable internal child to more possible pain and abuse. This early archetypal wounding could only be healed by another equally powerful archetype. It was almost as if an 'other' needed to experience the titanic emotions that John had endured and take that on, so that he could have an equally powerful experience of healing and wholeness. At just the 'right moment', it seems, *themis* energy fuelled an experience of heart-to-heart coherence between John and Pamela, which helped to reverse the destructive archetypal field. By being able to be there with him in that traumatized space and bear the destructive energies until the heart field shifted, Pamela could enable John to find a new experience of being.

Human beings are not born with mind–body coherence, although we are probably born with an inherent ability to develop it. Babies are born as pure blood-soul, hardwired to wail in distress and coo with delight to engage the person who is looking after them. Yet from the first hours of life, contemporary Western child-rearing dictates that each night this connection is severed. Almost immediately, the heart-soul communication is disrupted by the assumption that children should not sleep with their parents. There may be an even more serious consequence of this practice, since a baby may die suddenly and quietly in sleep, without evidence of trauma or illness. Crib death, or sudden infant death syndrome (SIDS), remains mysterious. Despite the advances in medical technologies and sophisticated pediatric care, the United States has the highest incidence in the world: two deaths for every thousand live births, which is ten times higher than the rate in Japan, and one hundred times that in Hong Kong. What the statistics show is that the societies with the lowest incidence of SIDS are the ones in which parent and infant habitually sleep together. In some such countries the syndrome is virtually unknown.[13]

Why should this be? James McKenna and his colleagues have studied how babies sleep in the natural environment prepared for them over millions of years of human development – maternal proximity: 'The temporal unfolding of particular sleep stages and awake periods of the mother and infant become entwined. On a minute-to-minute basis, throughout the night, much sensory communication is occurring between them.' If this research is correct, body-to-body communication between infant and parent may actually help to keep a sleeping baby alive. McKenna notes that 'the steady piston of an adult heart and the regular tidal sweeps of breath coordinate the ebb and flow of young internal rhythms'. Here is blood-soul communication at its purest. When this early learning between mother and child is severed at night, how much more must each child need to do to help restore the connection in the light of day? It is hard to know how much damage is done by this custom that undermines blood-soul communication even in infancy, but it is probably fair to say that it may be the beginning of Western training for the mind–body split.[14]

This chapter has been looking at some of the ways in which the split can be healed when the language of the blood-soul is relearned. Here is another, this time drawn not from the scientific laboratory or analytical consulting room, but from the heart and mind of a poet. Billy Collins, the former American poet laureate, gives a beautiful guide to how people can turn mind–body discordance into an appreciative state which welcomes those seemingly dis-ruptive urgings from the blood-soul. In this poem, the blood-soul is imaged as a barking dog, or that animal instinct which will not be ignored.

Another reason why I don't keep a gun in the house

The neighbors' dog will not stop barking.
He is barking the same high, rhythmic bark
that he barks every time they leave the house.
They must switch him on on their way out.

The neighbors' dog will not stop barking.
I close all the windows in the house
and put on a Beethoven symphony full blast
but I can still hear him muffled under the music,
barking, barking, barking,

and now I can see him sitting in the orchestra,
his head raised confidently as if Beethoven
had included a part for barking dog.

When the record finally ends he is still barking,
sitting there in the oboe section barking,
his eyes fixed on the conductor who is
entreating him with his baton

while the other musicians listen in respectful
silence to the famous barking dog solo,
that endless coda that first established
Beethoven as an innovative genius.[15]

This poem conjures the psychological experience of moving from a discordant state to a creative resonant one. Psychologically, the 'barking dog', may initially appear as a persistent mood, a physiological symptom, or an unbidden life event. Diana's 'barking dog', for instance, was hallucination and dissociation. Since the poet's barking dog is in the neighbour's house, there is the sense that it is close to him but not yet a part of his being. His present ego structure tries to keep it out by closing all the apparent access points. His mind is closed. When that doesn't work, he next tries a sophisticated diversion, a Beethoven symphony. But even this grand distraction doesn't work. At this point, the poet's ego structure is rigid and patriarchal like the mythic Ouranos and Kronos: it wants to repress the new in order to maintain the status quo. But then there is a wondrous shift. An attitude of openness, maybe even appreciation for this new, if initially distressing, material comes in. The 'dog' is invited in and takes centre stage with the oboes, the instruments that tune the whole orchestra. The old conductor, representing that part of the psyche that wants to hold on to the known order, entreats the dog with the baton. But the musicians, the parts of the psyche that know about rhythms and resonance, sit in respectful silence, resonating with a creative act of genius. And the poet has been profoundly changed.

This chapter has so far explored the power of the heart field, seeking out parallels between emerging scientific knowledge, ancient intuitions and experiences of *thymos*, the blood- or heart-soul, and what this book describes as *themis* energy. The analogies may also, however, be taken further, to involve other bodily organs than the heart and another ancient understanding. Science has validated clusters of neurons near major organs such as the stomach, lungs, kidneys, and intestines; these regulate the organs they serve and have also been called 'little brains'. There are some striking parallels here with the ancient Tantric system of kundalini yoga, which was based on seven energy centres, or chakras, within the human body. These chakras, shown in Figure 4.5, appear to correspond to some of the 'little brains' of the major organs.

The Sanskrit word 'kundalini' means literally 'she who is coiled'. This is the sleeping serpent coiled at the base of the spine, *kundalini-shatki*, or 'serpent power' – the creative force of the feminine itself. The purpose of the discipline of kundalini yoga is to awaken the serpent, and enable her to ascend through the seven chakras to the union of Shiva and Shakti, the very personifications of the great complementarity of 'masculine' and 'feminine' energies, bringing the adept ever nearer to a transformation of consciousness. Importantly, tantric philosophy emphasized that this process did not transcend the body. On the contrary, the adept's sensuous or emotional faculties must rather be cultivated and expanded, together with the dimensions of the mind.[16]

To draw parallels between these processes and those of Western psychological development seems irresistible, and their similarities across time and space can seem to confirm the archetypal nature of the energy they represent.

Figure 4.5 The path of the *kundalini*. Used by permission of Anna Goldmuntz.

There are dangers here: the two systems grew out of radically different under-standings of the nature of consciousness, and the Eastern understanding of the subtle body is very different to the Western approach to the actual one. Jung himself, who was to make much of the parallels, was sometimes at least properly circumspect about how far they should be taken. Although the comparison seemed to him thoroughly plausible, he emphasized that it was 'merely an analogy'. Far too many Europeans, he thought, were inclined to carry Eastern ideas and methods unexamined into their occidental mentality, to the advantage of neither.[17]

Nevertheless, both kundalini yoga and *themis* consciousness do seem to speak of a transformative process within the body which is fuelled by the divine feminine and her 'serpent power'. For all his cautions, Jung came to understand the experience and understanding as a description of the process of individuation. He saw the chakra centres as mandalas which connected powerful physiological and psychic experiences, and the kundalini as an autonomous process that arises out of the unconscious to use the individual for the development of higher states of consciousness. For him, the ancient yogic system threw light on the sometimes strange symptoms that patients could experience. When the kundalini begins to rise, he thought, it can manifest as 'something absolutely unrecognisable, which can show, say, as fear, as a neurosis, a symptom, or apparently also as vivid interest; but it must be something which is superior to your will. . . . [I]]f that living spark, that urge, that need, gets you by the neck, then you cannot turn back; and you have to face the music. . . . *Kundalini* is the divine urge.'[18]

As kundalini, this compelling urge, rises through the seven chakra centres, images and interpretations accrue, and even the outline of these which follows may help to illuminate the process of transformation and add to knowledge of the language of the blood-soul.

Muladhara, literally 'root support', is the lowest centre, located in the perineal region and traditionally associated with the earth. Sleeping in *muladhara* is the kundalini, coiled around the darkened lingam, an image of the supreme masculine energy personified by the god Shiva. So the divine masculine and feminine energies are united in the unconscious, but only *in potentia*. Jung saw this chakra as representing everyday Western consciousness, where we are aware of everyday 'reality', but where the 'gods' remain asleep.

Svadhisthana, 'own-standing centre', is connected with water. Found near the bladder, the intestines, and reproductive organs, it represents the sexual centre and the stirring of the sexual energies.

Manipura, which translates as 'fullness of jewels', is known as the fire centre. It corresponds to the solar plexus, the stomach and the diaphragm. Jung describes this third chakra as the emotional centre – a whirlpool of passions, instincts, and desires. When *manipura* is awakened, there may be emotional flare-ups, explosions, or sudden weeping about long-past events. Here the importance of the information coming from the instincts and emotions is brought to consciousness.

Anahata, situated in the region of the heart, means 'unstuck'. This is the region of the heart-brain, documented by present day neurocardiology. In the kundalini system, this fourth chakra is also associated with the lungs and air, because the heart is embedded in the lungs and its whole activity is closely associated with them. Jung described this as the chakra of thinking and feeling, the beginning of reflection, of values and ideas. When this 'heart-brain' is awakened, there is a movement from simply reacting to the emotions to asking 'Why am I behaving like this?' Jung reckoned that humankind as a whole had more or less reached *anahata*, and thought that the next three chakras were difficult to describe because so few had reached these levels.

Vishuddha, meaning 'centre of purity,' is situated in the throat. When *vishuddha* is awakened, the individual perspective on the world is transcended. Jung describes it as finding a symbolical bridge between the most abstract ideas of physics and the most abstract ideas of analytical psychology, and then experiencing the psychical essences or substances as the fundamental essences of the world. In *vishuddha*, there is also an awareness of the deep connection between what is inside oneself and what is outside. As we saw in Chapter 3, Diana's first drawing of herself alone, with the diamond at her throat, signalled an awakening of this chakra and the psychic development it implies.

Ajna, located between the eyebrows, means 'command centre'. Also known as the 'third eye', *Ajna* is a state of complete consciousness that includes everything – consciousness of energy itself. The sense of self, or ego, disappears completely; the psychical is no longer a content in us, but we become contents of it. In such an extended consciousness, all the chakras would be simultaneously experienced. Now the lingam reappears, but instead of appearing darkened, as it did in *muladhara*, it is now fully white. Jung suggests that as kundalini awakens this chakra, an experience of the divine Shiva becomes conscious in a *unio mystica*, as the masculine and feminine energies are consciously reunited.

Sahasrara means 'the lotus of the thousand petals', and is located at the top of the skull. In Sanskrit literature, this centre is described as 'lustrous', 'whiter than the full moon', 'shedding a constant and profuse stream of nectar'. Jung describes the *sahasrara* centre as reaching the understanding that there is no object, no God, nothing but Brahman. It is the state of achieving nirvana.[19]

So for Jung, kundalini yoga represented a rich storehouse of symbolic depictions of inner experience and of the individuation process in particular. He found that when this process is initiated in the individual, very often the symbol of the serpent appears in their dreams or other imagery.[20] This was certainly true for Diana, as we have seen. It was also true for Jennifer.

When Jennifer began analysis, she was concerned about a series of physical symptoms which seemed to have no obvious physiological cause. She was a successful attorney in a very demanding law firm, but suffered from endometriosis (a condition of the uterus), stomach problems, and frequent throat infections. Visits to the doctor and various medications had not helped to relieve these physical symptoms, so she had decided to try a Jungian approach.

It quickly became clear that one of the things lacking for Jennifer was any semblance of an inner life. All her energy had been focused outward into tasks to accomplish and goals to achieve. But her blood-soul had rebelled, throwing up a painful variety of physical symptoms that made it more and more difficult for her to continue on this driven path. During the course of analysis, she was encouraged to bring her dreams, draw pictures of her physical symptoms, and describe her feelings, emotions, and experiences.

As a connection with her inner world began to develop, Jennifer had the following dream:

I am lying in bed when a large green snake appears running though my body. Its

tail comes out between my legs and its head emerges through my face. It is
undulating through my body in a soothing almost hypnotic way. It feels like the
most natural thing in the world.

When Jennifer awakened from the dream, she realized that the snake was still there. She enjoyed the feel of it for a few minutes, but then became afraid that it was not going to go away. She got up, walked around, and felt relieved when it disappeared.

In describing the dream in analysis, Jennifer seemed quite embarrassed and a little concerned about how this 'hallucination' of a snake would be received. However, when she learned of the ancient system of kundalini and how it might relate to the symptoms that had manifested in her body, this rational lawyer began to see the snake as 'evidence' of the reality of the objective psyche. With this deepened awareness, she was able to develop a rich relationship with the process that was emerging from within her. Once she became aware of her own 'snake woman', her physical symptoms disappeared as her mind–body split began to heal. Her understanding of the law also took on a more universal meaning as she began to work for ways to heal communities rather than use the legal system to punish perceived violations of the law.

The appearance of Jennifer's kundalini snake suggests that openings had occurred in the chakra areas where her symptoms had appeared – in the second chakra, associated with the uterus; the third, associated with the stomach; and the fifth, associated with the throat. The dream image of the snake leaving through the face suggests an awakening of new consciousness, corresponding to the area between the fifth and sixth chakras. Jennifer gained a new awareness of the need for healing the mind–body split within herself and the need for healing in the community as well. This is the area of the *vishuddha* chakra, in which, according to Western commentators, inner and outer became intimately related.

Kundalini yoga is only one of a number of ancient systems that have expressed the wisdom of the body and the blood-soul. The earliest references to systems in the body can be found in the Vedas, the most ancient scriptures of India, and this knowledge formed the basis for the later teachings of the Upanishads, Agamas, Tantras, and Samhitas, and especially the texts belonging to the hatha yoga tradition. It became an integral part of the esoteric teachings of Tibetan Buddhism, Chinese Taoism, the spirituality of certain American Indian tribes, shamans, and the bushmen of Africa. Transformations of body and spirit also underlie the spiritual experiences of Christian mystics and Sufi masters. The whole process of alchemy, with its key relationship between masculine and feminine, adept and *soror mystica*, was about these transformations; indeed, Jung called alchemy 'a Western form of yoga'.[21] The dynamics of transformation are also imaged in the ancient Pelasgian creation myth, and the dance of creation between the feminine principle, the Goddess of All Things, and the serpent that she manifests from her own energy. All these great mythological systems speak of the language of the blood-soul, and still find their echoes in contemporary life. Diana's drawing of the 'snakewomen' signalled the beginning of her own process of transformation, and her mandala, which marked its culmination, showed a new balance of masculine and feminine energies.

So the wisdom of the body is more ancient and vastly more sophisticated than the rational mind alone can know, and ignoring its messages can lead to psychological and physiological distress. Its language may only now be becoming once more accessible to consciousness. But its communications are stored in the body's information system and can be reached through 'irrational' means, like paying attention to dreams and images that arise from the unconscious and working with memories. This is no 'new' discovery, for there was a time when such communications were revered and honoured at the very centre of the world. The next chapter continues to explore the ancient wisdom of the blood-soul as it manifested on a cultural level in ancient Delphi, and further explores how it may still be relevant and needed today, not just by individuals, but by whole communities.

Chapter 5

The voice of the goddess

From the beginning, Themis was at the centre of the world. And just as she drew together the gods of Olympus, as the oracle of Earth herself she drew humans to that centre to find the answer to their own deepest questions:

> I count the grains of sand on the beach and measure the sea;
> I understand the speech of the dumb and hear the voiceless.[1]

The stories of Delphi and Themis as its oracle bring mythology into recorded human history and link both with the traces of human lives buried over millennia. So these stories can tell more about the universal and enduring human yearning for connection with the deep source of life and wisdom, and how this has been sought in the outer as well as the inner world. They can illuminate too, in microcosm, a collective setting in which individuals have been and still are embedded: they trace a movement of Western consciousness away from its connection with the deep wisdom of the earth, the realm of the heart-soul and Themis, towards the Apollonian heights of spirit-soul and intellect. And the story of Delphi itself, from the wealth of its glory to its corruption and decline, can perhaps tell too of what happens, in both individuals and in communities, when their connection with the blood-soul is lost.

They say that Zeus once let fly two eagles, one from his right hand and one from his left, to circle the globe and discover its centre. They met at Delphi. There he set the great stone omphalos, the world's navel, and created the temple to Apollo that was to become, after his own at Olympia, the greatest of all the Greek shrines and its most powerful oracle.[2]

But Zeus's was a much later story, and the place to which the eagles were drawn had already been a powerhouse of wisdom since time began. In the beginning, the voice of the oracle came not from the intellectual clarity of Apollo, 'the one who shoots from afar', but from deep within the most ancient natural structures. They say the first oracle at the centre of the world was Gaia, Mother Earth herself, and the second, by her gift, was her daughter Themis, so close to her that they would be known as 'one person, though of various names'. The grandeur of the site, clinging to the rock below the great peaks of Parnassus on a gorge that plunges 2000 feet to a beautiful valley, with the Gulf of Corinth beyond, embodies the power of Earth, that natural force who out of her own self, as Hesiod tells, bore the great mountains and the barren swollen sea. In those days, long before Delphi itself was founded, the oracle spoke from the Corycian cave, high on Mount Parnassus, guarded by Gaia's child, the serpent Python. Later the goddess was worshipped near Delphi itself, beneath the Castalian spring, which wells up from a deep ravine in the mountain, and at the very heart of its sacred site. This is where myth comes into history: archaeological excavations over the last 120 years have once more opened earth's secrets, and their evidence suggests that goddess worship at both the Corycian cave and in the area of Delphi itself was continuous over 2000 years.[3]

In a statuette from Delphi that dates from this ancient time, the goddess is enthroned on a three-legged chair (Figure 5.1). The image celebrates the numinous power of fertility and childbearing, and it is universal: versions of it have been found from Babylonia to Crete, from Egypt to India and Central America.[4]

Both above in the mountain and below by the spring, the wisdom of the oracle came from within Earth herself. The very name 'Delphi' is connected with an old word for 'womb', and earth's womb was opened by the convulsions of her own deep movements, the quakes and rockslides which could bring danger and destruction as well as protecting later settlements from invaders. The prophecies that issued from her were, as Ovid said, 'the voice of Fate'.[5] These had less to do with foretelling the future, perhaps, than speaking of a place in which past, present and future are eclipsed to tell what profoundly is.

The oracular voice at Delphi is long silenced. But the psychological truths it embodied are still part of human nature. Legend says that its power was first discovered when local goats began to reel from the inspirational fumes that rose from a fissure in the earth; it was when intoxicated by these fumes that the priestess of the oracle was able to give its pronouncements. As then, so throughout history: the use of drugs that release consciousness to experience fantasies, imaginings and a connection with 'something beyond' has its roots in the universal search for connection with the divine.

Today's consciousness can bring that search inwards: people may seek the connection in their own deep places where once they sought it by devotion to distant gods. But *themis* can still help human beings to learn who they deeply are and the natural law by which they live. The oracle brought together humans, the divine and the ancestral underworld – in psychological language, the conscious mind and the deep unconscious from which it grew. Diana's 'oracle', as Chapters 2 and 3 have shown, spoke in her own dreams, drawings and imaginings. As depth psychologists from Freud onwards have emphasized, dreams, produced in a state of unconsciousness but remembered

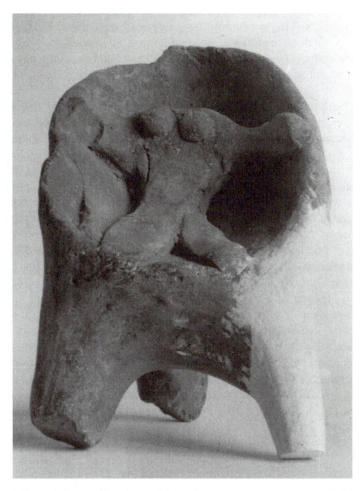

Figure 5.1 Ancient Themis, daughter of Earth. Photographer: kein Eintrag, DAI-Neg.-No. D-DAI-ATH-Delphi 133.

in consciousness, are a particularly privileged bridge to deeper places and truths. The ancients knew that their gods could speak through dreams as well as oracles, and the similarities between the two have been often remarked.

Some would say this similarity includes their obscurity. The ambiguity and apparent equivocation of the Delphic oracle was much debated in its own time and has been by scholars since, just as dreams have been. Freud found them so deliberately obscure that they demanded a theory of meaning behind ostensible meaning to unravel the 'disguised expression of a repressed wish' that they encoded: 'a dream without condensation, distortion, dramatisation, above all without wish fulfilment, surely hardly deserves the name'. Yet for others, the apparent obscurity of both dreams and oracles means simply that they are speaking in symbolic language of aspects of psyche that are not yet fully available to the rational, conscious mind, in an attempt to bring them to understanding. As the ancient Greek philosopher Heraclitus put it: 'The god whose oracle is at Delphi neither speaks nor remains silent, but gives signs.'[6]

Jung, like Freud, found that dreams were great educators about unconscious psychological processes. But his view of their educational method was a very different one. For him, dreams were 'the best possible representation for the moment for a fact as yet unknown'; they were '*part of nature*, which harbours no intention to deceive, but expresses something as best it can.' Socrates might have agreed. Told that the Delphic oracle had answered 'No' to an enquirer who asked if anyone was wiser than himself, his first reaction was not to enjoy the apparent compliment, but to ask, 'What does the god mean?' He set out to interview everyone he could find with a reputation for wisdom – politicians, poets, skilled craftsmen. And he concluded that the oracle meant that real wisdom belonged to the deity, and that the wisest man was the one, like Socrates himself, who best realized that.[7]

So the oracular voice, like the dream, can take humans on a pilgrimage to discover their own true nature and their relation to what for them is the divine: it has to do with both the process and the goal of the quest. The psychological energy that carries that search, the original oracular voice, is that of Themis herself, which bridges consciousness and the unconscious to call different psychic contents together into awareness. The oracle at Delphi offers a powerful image of that containing power, and something else as well: an evocation of the centre that holds the different contents in balance. So *themis* energy has to do with both the process and the goal of the search for greater self-understanding, and encompasses and focuses the interplay of different contents of psyche.

These are very much the qualities of what Jung called the Self, the central archetype that both orders psychic contents and enables consciousness to find meaning in them. 'This,' he said, 'is not only the centre but also the whole circumference which embraces both conscious and unconscious; it is the centre of this totality, just as the ego is the centre of consciousness.' Jung borrowed his definition from the thirteenth-century St Bonaventure's description of God as 'an intelligible sphere whose centre is everywhere and circumference is nowhere'. He quoted too the seventeenth-century Polish mystic Angelus Silesius: 'God is my centre when I close him in;/And my circumference when I melt in him.'[8] The manifestation of *themis* energy at Delphi gives another, far more ancient, expression to the idea, and in the story of Diana we can see its contemporary power. In her mandala (Figure 3.6, p.47), which came at the culmination of her analytical work as an image of her greater psychological wholeness, the ancient power of the serpent both bounded and focused her sense of herself. So *themis* energy has been a psychological constant across time and culture; it has been at work in individuals, as it was in Diana, and, as it was at Delphi, in whole communities as well.

For Jung, awareness of relationship between ego and Self was crucial to the individual work of becoming more whole. But that relationship is not always easy to sustain in the contemporary Western world, which has so often lost its sense of a link between the individual 'I' and 'something beyond' the mundane. The poet Yeats' perception can seem as relevant now as it was some 80 years ago:

> Things fall apart; the centre cannot hold;
> Mere anarchy is loosed upon the world,
> The blood-dimmed tide is loosed, and everywhere
> The ceremony of innocence is drowned. . . .[9]

Yet ego-dominated, rational, Western consciousness is also drawn by a sense of something beyond itself. However much formal religious commitment is falling in Western countries, surveys show that very many people still have a sense of a 'spiritual' dimension to life, and the burgeoning of different 'spiritual paths' shows the strength of yearning for a New Age beyond the everyday, one more personal and less 'out there'. One British study, for instance, after charting the decline of organized Christian observance and the rise of what it characterizes as 'subjective life spirituality', draws on similar work to conclude that it will indeed be possible to speak of the 'spiritual revolution' in the West within the next 30 years.[10]

In this nascent revolution, the imagery of *themis* energy as both centre and circumference still carries numinosity, not just for individuals but in societies. The mandala image that was so powerful for Diana holds collective value too. After the destruction of the World Trade Center on 11 September 2001, the Smithsonian Institution invited the Tibetan Buddhist monks of Drepung Loseling Monastery to lead prayer ceremonies and create sand mandalas in New York and Washington, where more than 45,000 people participated. Now the monks continue to travel in the United States and Europe 'for world healing', with their programmes of sacred music, dance and ceremony. And people are still drawn together to witness a precise enacting of the sacred imagery of centre and circumference, as the monks measure out in coloured sand the complexity of the mandala of Buddha Akshobhya, which has particularly to do with conflict resolution, protection and healing.[11]

Where in the West did the old wisdom go? Already by the eighth century BCE, human consciousness had moved on: now the oracular voice came no longer from Mother Earth or Themis, but from the dazzling rationality of the god who above all represents the capacity for abstract thought. Delphi became the greatest cult centre of Apollo, son of Zeus and Leto. Some say that Apollo's gaining of the oracle from Themis was entirely peaceful. At the beginning of Aeschylus's *Eumenides*, the oracle's priestess tells how, 'with the consent of Themis/ and with no violence done to any', the succession passed from the goddess to Phoebe, another child of Earth, who in turn gave it to Apollo as a birthday present.[12]

But others tell a far harsher tale. Apollo, they say, ranged all over the earth, searching for a place to found his oracle, and eventually came to what is now Delphi. Here he decided to build his beautiful temple. From the start, he had big plans for this oracular site: people would visit from the mainland of Greece, the wave-washed islands and even the whole of Europe. He found a beautifully flowing spring – and there the archer-god shot the great fat she-dragon, a 'calamity of blood', who had been the scourge of local humans and beasts. Or had she? This 'calamity of blood' was the Python, the guardian of the oracle. Even now Homer knew Delphi by the ancient name of Pytho which once honoured her power. But for Apollo's plan to succeed, the oracle's guardian had to be destroyed. This is what happened:

> the lord Apollo,
> who works from afar,
> let fly at her his strong arrow.
> Then, heavily, she lay there,
> racked with bitter pain,
> gasping for breath
> and rolling about on the ground.
> An unspeakable scream
> came into being,
> a more than mortal sound.
> All over the wood
> she writhed incessantly,
> now here, now there,
> and then
> life left her,
> breathing out blood.[13]

And that, they say, is how the place and the serpent were named 'Pytho' – not in honour, but because it means 'rotting', and the piercing power of Apollo made the monster rot away.[14]

The god acknowledged the enormity of his blood-crime, and the Pythian Games he instituted in atonement became a festival second in importance only to the games at Olympia. But the injury to the blood-soul could not be undone. Apollo's annexation of the oracle at Delphi is one of the defining moments in the development of Western consciousness. In the 'unspeakable scream' of the Python is the death-agony of feminine rule, now overwhelmed by the new masculine order. The way ahead was signposted: from now on it would be the dazzling capacities of conscious intellect that understood both past and future, while the deep natural knowledge that unites them both with the present would belong to what centuries later would be called 'the unconscious'. As the Python breathed out her life blood, the blood-soul and its heart connection gave place to the spirit-soul, and the Titan–Olympian split deepened.

As we saw in Chapter 1, this is a story whose essentials had already been foretold, when the Babylonian god Marduk had tortured and crushed the great primal sea-dragon Tiamat and created the earth from her lifeless body. The *Enuma Elish*, which tells this tale, would become the mythological root of all three patriarchal religions, and marked a radical shift in understanding: from a mother-goddess who *was* heaven and earth to a father-god who *made* them. 'The essential identity between creator and creation was broken', as Baring and Cashford say in *The Myth of the Goddess*, 'and a fundamental dualism was born from their separation, the dualism that we know as spirit and nature.'[15]

So began – and so with Apollo's triumph began again in Delphi – the denigration of the body, instincts and matter itself, of all that was associated with 'the feminine', which has finally contributed so significantly to today's personal and collective disorders. The snake or serpent, image of the primordial energy, which had appeared unbidden in Diana's drawing as Atargatis the snake-goddess (Figure 2.2, p.28), became identified with evil and destruction.

Again and again, in different times and places, the story is retold. Western consciousness has been shaped by the Judeo-Christian story of the serpent's temptation of Eve: the eventual identification of the feminine with the source of man's suffering would become so complete that Eve would sometimes be portrayed with the same face as the serpent. In later Olympian times, the Libyan princess Medusa whose blood carried the goddess's ancient power over both life and death became the paralysing monster with hideous snaky hair, slain by heroic Perseus. Echoes from Delphi tell the same tale. Some say the guardian of the oracle who gave the place its name was not Pytho, but Delphyne; yet the second became no less horrible a monster, no less deserving of destruction than the first. Others say that the oracle was once given by the most ancient of all the Sibyls, daughter of Zeus and Lamia. But Lamia, another beautiful princess of Libya, became a foul monster in her turn, her name meaning both 'lecherous' and 'gluttonous' as she devoured her lovers and young children. Later, she would multiply into a whole species of beautiful women who were serpents from the waist down; in the Middle Ages they were synonymous with witches, and as the poet Keats would later tell, destroyed their husbands on their wedding night. So the deathly snakewoman, that deadly feminine power, wove and hissed her way through Western legend.[16]

In Delphi, Mother Earth fought back against the annexation of her sacred place. They say she was so enraged at Apollo's usurpation of Themis that she bypassed his power entirely by giving humans their own oracular power, sending them dreams that told them of things past and things to come. But Apollo, only a baby still in this version of events, ran to Zeus and gripping his father's golden throne with his chubby but so determined little hand demanded the return of his monopoly. Zeus laughed to see how the shrewd child had already reckoned what he had to lose by way of gold from worshippers; he snatched back the dream-power from humans and gave imperious little Apollo what he asked for. His plans for Delphi had perhaps to be modified, for the sacred places were already dedicated to Dionysus, god of vegetation and fertility, who each year died to be born again. The two gods continued to be worshipped – and in that holding together of the forces of nature and culture, irrationality and reason, maybe the power of Themis, who brings together disparate energies and holds them in balance, still held some sway. Yet the energy that was once known to come from the deep feminine places had irrevocably passed to the realm of the masculine gods.[17]

Delphi began to change. The first shrines, built of the natural substances of bay leaves, wax and feathers, were gradually replaced by a huge magnificence of temples, shrines and monuments that attested to the finest arts of civilisation. The great omphalos, the navel-stone that marked the entrance to earth's womb, was once named for the she-dragon in her guise as Omphale. Now it marked her tomb, and so became symbol of the great circle of life, from birth to death, which was once in the goddess's charge. The sacred rumour mill turned again, and this became the tomb not just of the Python but of Dionysus as well: even the masculine connection with the earth energies now seemed dead. One more turn, and here was another sacred stone: the one that Kronos swallowed in place of the infant Zeus. So the stones of Delphi tell the story of the honouring of spirit-soul over blood-soul in the development of Western consciousness.[18]

Sacred stones have huge power: across time and place, humans have venerated them as power centres of the energy that fuels the world. Sometimes they appear suddenly from earth below, her very bones; sometimes from heaven above, fragments of the upper universe. So their origin is mysterious and ungraspable. Yet at the same time they are stable and solid to the touch. Like the gods whose energy they so often contain or conduct, their nature is unchanging. And at the same time, they are transformative – as worshippers before the phallic lingam of the Hindu god Shiva know to this day. They can seem insignificant, simply the makings of a larger landscape, yet they are the very stuff of the buildings which from ancient times have drawn humans in their search for contact with their divinities. They can stand metaphor for those divinities: Christ, says St Peter, drawing on the words of the Psalmist, is the stone that was rejected and has become the corner-stone (1 Pet. 2, 4–7).

From the piled up cairns that signpost the way through a world of landscapes to the tombstones over graves, stones mark the human journey. They bring individuals to focus on their own centre, and they still mark the world's centre for believers, just as the omphalos did at Delphi. Pilgrims to Mecca journey to the Ka'bah, the earthly granite House of God which is directly below its heavenly counterpart, and know the Black Stone embedded in its eastern corner as 'the corner-stone of the House' and its most sacred and powerful object. Jews assemble and pray at the Eastern Wall of the Temple Mount in Jerusalem, their most hallowed place because of its proximity to the Holy of Holies, from which the divine presence has never departed.[19]

Even in a heartland of contemporary technology, the power of the stone can still touch. In 2005, a major London hospital that cares for people of all faiths and none placed a huge, polished stone in front of the main entrance to its new buildings: made of Brazilian granite and entitled 'Monolith and Shadow', its patterns look like magnified clusters of cells. The idea, says the hospital, was to foster a sense of welcome and reassurance in place of the traditional clinical atmosphere. The chief nurse emphasized the healing effects of this and cited increasing evidence that a welcoming atmosphere improved patient well-being and staff morale, and could even speed recovery.[20]

After the death of the old gods in the West, the power of sacred stones continued to reverberate. In the mysterious laboratories of the alchemists, right up until the seventeenth century, the search continued for the philosopher's stone: this was the *lapis* which for many was also Christ, and which would unite masculine, feminine and all opposites in 'the instinct of truth' – a search that Jung would see as metaphor for the psychological urge towards the Self. In the outer world, the shape of sacred stones was still outlined by the domes and arches of the buildings which now contained the energy of the divine. But the image and perception of that sacred energy had changed. At the start of the fourth century, the Roman Emperor Constantine, led they say by a dream, declared Christianity the official religion of the Empire, and had Delphi pillaged. In the great domes and arches of Santa Costanza, the mausoleum for his daughter that Constantine had built in Rome, the outlined shape of the sacred omphalos can still be discerned. But as arch and dome reach up to the heavens to leave the earth behind, this is also a powerful image for the entombment of the feminine principle itself.[21]

Yet still the earth yields up her secrets, and Figure 5.2 is an omphalos, image of the navel stone set by Zeus himself to mark the centre of the world where his eagles met. Found in twentieth-century excavations at Delphi, it is the first object that visitors see when they visit its museum: a Hellenistic or early Roman copy, the guidebook says, of the original sacred stone in the Temple of Apollo. It may even, it suggests, be the stone that Pausanias saw on his visit to Delphi in the second century CE.

Pausanias did not seem much impressed by the omphalos, saying simply that it was made of white stone. The stone that seemed more lastingly important, certainly from his account, was the one that Kronos swallowed in place of the infant Zeus. Even when Pausanias visited, all those centuries later, this was still oiled every day, garlanded, and offered unwound wool at all the festivals. So the dynastic foundation myth of the Olympian gods was placed at the very centre of the world, where once *themis* energy had had an earthly home.[22]

Figure 5.2 The Omphalos marks the centre of the world. Delphi Archaeological Museum,
Hellenic Ministry of Culture – Archaeological Receipts Fund.

Yet this was the only one of Apollo's temples in all of Greece in which he
was served not by a priest, but a priestess, the Pythia, and her first invocation
was not to the god, but to Earth and then Themis.[23] As late as the fourth
century BCE, the Pythia was portrayed as Themis herself.

In Figure 5.3, the goddess is shown in a vase painting, with her mandala
and its eight-pointed star, sitting on the tripod placed across the fissure in the
earth from which the mantic fumes arose. The three-legged support had a
practical purpose: some say those fumes were so powerful that humans who
ingested them would sometimes reel over the huge cliff to their death in the
Gulf of Corinth, so a woman was installed on a stool to catch the prophecies
while supplicants kept their lives. But the tripod also recalls the ancient

Figure 5.3 Themis as the Oracle of Delphi: Fifth century BCE vase painting. Bildarchiv
Preussischer Kulturbesitz/Art Resource, NY.

three-legged armchair on which the ancient fertility goddess was enthroned
(Figure 5.1) and evokes her triple nature as ruler of birth, death and regeneration, heaven, earth and the underworld. In the image, the tripod is also a
container, holding the priestess and the three-fold power she mediates. This
vessel has a parallel in the ancient Chinese *ting*, the three-legged ritual cauldron which held sacrifices to the ancestors and the divine, and symbolized
nourishment; to this day the *ting* is one of the 14 Precious Things, a Chinese
symbol of good fortune.[24]

What happened to the ancient three-fold feminine energy that so powerfully
drew private individuals and public statesmen to Delphi for so long? As time
went on, the values of the blood-soul became increasingly lost in outward
observance. Although the historian Ephorus, writing in the fourth century
BCE, knew that Delphi had been founded by Themis and Apollo together,

already he was stressing their moral intent in terms of outer regulation rather than inner knowing. The deities, he said, had desired to benefit the human race by 'summoning humanity to civilisation and rebuking it, partly by giving oracular responses, partly by issuing commands and prohibitions and again by refusing altogether to admit to the temple certain individuals'. But this moral intent also dimmed as its many temples, monuments and treasuries – baby Apollo was right! – turned it into a hugely wealthy showcase for the civilized skills. That display took some governing: most of the few historical oracles that survive concern the conduct of rituals, founding of cults and nature of sacrifices. Above all, Delphi became concerned with affairs of state, the magnet for rulers seeking guidance on the auspicious founding of new colonies and the gods' blessings on their enterprise. The treasuries that lined the Sacred Way, dedicated by the city-states, were solid evidence of its political importance – and its apparent impartiality too, as the deeds celebrated in one had often been achieved at the bloody expense of the state whose treasury was right alongside.[25]

So 'Nothing in excess', one of the sayings of the legendary Seven Wise Men inscribed on a temple, was more honoured in the material breach than the observance. Yet 'Know thyself', the most famous saying, remained the injunction to the countless, unrecorded individuals who probably made up the majority of the oracle's suppliants throughout its long history – and so recalled them to their inner world and their own blood-soul. Sometimes private affairs had public consequences, as they did so devastatingly when the oracle foretold the whole tragedy of Oedipus and his kin. Few families would remain as known to posterity as this one. But the questions about marriage, succession, enterprise and devotion that most suppliants brought were for them no less pressing.

For them, the oracle's focus was not on the outer world of prestige and power. Who, asks one ostentatiously wealthy suppliant from Magnesia, most pleases the gods? The desired response can perhaps be guessed. But what the oracle tells him is that despite his own huge offerings, the gods are best pleased with a farmer who from his meagre living gives both regularly and exactly. Who, asks a proud and affluent ruler of Lydia, is the happiest of men? Not one like you, says the oracle, but a man who lives contentedly and faithfully on his tiny plot and has never travelled in his life. And who, asks a Spartan famous for his knowledge, is the wisest? Not you, the oracle replies, but a man who turns out to be a god-fearing peasant in a remote part of the country.[26]

So *themis* energy still drew people back to their own centre, their own inner truth, as it took them beyond the outer trappings of wealth and learning to remind them of other values. In Jung's terms, this is very like the operation of the Self, that *diras necessitas* which is a constant challenge to the conscious ego: '[t]he ego must make itself conscious of its claim', as he said, 'and the self must cause the ego to renounce it.' This challenge may be painful. For one recent commentator, the Self is even experienced as the 'violent Other'.

'The self is "violent",' says Lucy Huskinson, 'because it is experienced as an overwhelming force that violates the self-containment of the ego, and forces the ego, often against its will, into a new identity.' However painful this may sometimes be, this ego-Self dialectic seems to be the way to a greater sense of psychic wholeness; without it, there is a loss of meaning and purpose. This continual push–pull between rational consciousness and the sense of 'something beyond' can bring a sense of diminution: 'The experience of the self is always a defeat for the ego,' says Jung. Yet in that defeat there is also a sense that something has been gained, a fuller understanding reached.[27]

In Delphi, the connection to the Self became progressively weaker. The oracle's power and influence eventually brought its own corruption, and the story of its decline can show what happens when connection with Themis's 'right order' and natural law is lost. The oracle's pronouncements became political: the priests who had now taken over from Apollo's unique priestess were suspected of taking bribes. Already by the third century BCE, the oracle's public influence was in decline, and its religious significance was waning: philosophers attributed its voice not to Apollo, but to lesser daemons who, like mortals, were subject to change and death. By the time Pausanias visited, in the second century CE, even the oracle's beginnings were attributed to Apollo. The Python lost its feminine origins too: the Christian church father Clement of Alexandria reported that *he* was worshipped at Delphi, *his* bones and teeth believed to be preserved in the kettle that stood on the sacred tripod. In time, even the tripod was destroyed in plundering by barbarians and looting by Roman emperors: some still say that the Serpentine Column brought to ancient Constantinople and now standing in the Hippodrome in Istanbul is actually one of its legs.[28]

As Christianity became the religion of the Empire, the oracle finally failed. Its last utterance was said to be in the middle of the fourth century, for the Emperor Julian the Apostate, who had tried to revive it:

> Tell the King; the fairwrought hall has fallen to the ground. No longer has Phoebus a hut, nor a prophetic laurel, nor a spring that speaks. The water of speech even is quenched.[29]

Yet the energy of the goddess was not entirely lost: the oracular feminine voice survived into the Christian middle ages and beyond. The Sibyl of Delphi, of whom Pausanias had written as the original priestess, was one of the most famous of these ten prophetic women, the only religious figures from the pagan era to find a place in Christian doctrine. That place was hard won. When the Cumean Sibyl offered to sell her nine books of oracles to Tarquin the Proud, the last King of Rome, he dismissed her. She burned three of the priceless books. The next day, she returned and offered the six remaining volumes for the original price. The king sent her packing. She burned three more books. On the third day, she offered all that was left of her invaluable oracle for the same price again. This time, the king paid up, and the books were preserved to be consulted at times of crisis. But if the message honoured, the messenger was not. By medieval times, in a familiar story of denigration of the once great power of the feminine, the Cumean Sibyl had become associated with sexuality and sensuous enticements of every kind. More generally though, the Christian church took the Sibyls' words as authentic guides to the coming Christian salvation or doom. With the invention of printing, these words reached a wider and wider public, and the Sibyls appeared in paintings and sacred places, most famously in Michelangelo's Sistine Chapel.[30]

Beyond this echo of the oracular feminine voice, the Delphic oracle also left one abiding ideal. From as early as 1100 BCE, the sanctuary had been the centre of the Amphictyonic League, an association of 12 tribes, each with different numbers of city-states. These included both Athens and Sparta, and also others far less important. But within the League, no state, whatever its size or strength, had more authority than any other. So Delphi enshrined a principle of cooperation and respect which had to do with something other than the dominance of the powerful, and it offered a vision of governance that respects the small voice as much as it does the great. This drawing together of different elements in the search for a greater harmony and wholeness is precisely the realm of Themis, and her oracular energy fostered the principle in another way as well. At a time when Greece was plagued by civil wars, the Delphic oracle was asked for healing, and the priestess Pythia decreed that there should be a restoration of the Olympic Games, originally set up to celebrate Zeus's overthrow of his father Kronos. The games were restored, and with them the Olympic Truce, which guaranteed safe passage to all athletes, artists and their families, as well as ordinary pilgrims. For the period of the games, enmities of state were set aside. This ideal, in theory at least, remains alive today, as the Olympic Charter continues to celebrate the qualities of 'body, will and mind', and proclaims 'respect for universal, fundamental ethical principles'.[31]

So the stories of Themis at Delphi still have an after-life. They also still tell of how *themis* energy may work in both individuals and communities – and what may happen when connection with the goddess is lost. Her oracle drew individuals to a deeper knowledge of themselves and their own deep centre. It brought together representatives of power and simple peasants, mighty states and modest governments, and decreed mutual respect and peace in place of enmity and warfare. The distance between this vision and today's realities may seem unbridgeable. But as Chapters 7 and 8 explore, there are also places where *themis* energy may be seen at work, not just in individuals but between them, and in communities as well. Before that, however, the next chapter traces what happened to Themis's 'right order' and divine justice over the centuries – and the deep yearning to reconnect to it.

Chapter 6

Yearning for justice

Across the continents, from Manhattan to Melbourne to Mumbai, one Olympian above all remains insistently present. On top of civic buildings, inside courts of law, even on desk lamps for lawyers and advertisements for television shows, the figure of Justice is instantly recognizable by her sword, her scales and very often her blindfold too. This is Themis, the personification of divine justice and order. Paradoxically, the most hidden of the Olympian deities is now the most visible: it seems that the contemporary world, in all its administrative complexities, still needs reminders of this energy (Figures 6.1 and 6.2).

As we have seen, *themis* consciousness brings together the Olympians who are images of different psychological energies, and draws humans to the centre of their own inner world to discover the truth of their lives. It also brings these qualities into the work of collective human affairs. Themis is the deity who 'summons and dissolves the parliaments of men'. The classicist Jane Harrison, her great admirer, calls her the very spirit of the agora, the marketplace which was also the centre of government in classical Greece: she sees the goddess as personifying the energy which brings and binds people together, the collective conscience, the social sanction which underlies concepts of law and justice, and the source of religion itself. This power to summon and bind together is not confined to the official assemblies of which Harrison writes, but can operate wherever humans honour the goddess in their need to come together in peace. The people of the great trading centre of Aigina, for instance, turned to Themis above all deities to protect and foster their dealings with the many strangers who came to their shores.[1]

Yet if the image of Themis as personification of Justice is still widespread, the energy it represents can seem grievously lacking in today's troubled world. Where is the justice in the harshness of inequalities between nations and individuals, the persecutions of millions caught up in conflicts that are none of their making, the systematic denial of human rights on which huge governments depend? The machinery of justice is flawed, and Justice herself suffers. At the beginning of 2006, to take just one instance, the cover of the American magazine *Harper's* showed her blindfolded, anguished and

Figure 6.1 Themis as Justice at the Old Bailey, London. Photonews Service Ltd, London.

straining, her sword eclipsed in shadow and her hand clutching tortuously at her scales. This picture illustrated an article which argued that senior US officers who created the culture of abuse of Iraqi prisoners at Abu Ghraibe had got off scot-free, while junior soldiers who were acting within that culture had been scapegoated, court-martialled and punished.[2]

Where did justice go? The question is an ancient one. Even when the gods ruled on Olympus, all was far from right with the world. The Golden Age was only a nostalgic memory. Then men had lived like gods themselves in the bounty of nature, free from work and sadness, never ageing, lively limbed right up to the moment when death came gentle as a sleep. But ever since, it had been downhill all the way. Now it was the age not of gold, nor silver nor even bronze, but of iron. In this Iron Age, humankind worked and grieved unceasingly, and all harmony was lost in lies and envy, quarrels and war. Natural bonds were broken, as children pried into their parents' horoscopes, impatient for their inheritance; spouses could not wait for each other's deaths

Figure 6.2 Themis as Justice at the U.S. Supreme Court, Washington, D.C. Photograph by Gabe Brammer and Bob Brammer, Iowa Attorney General's Office.

and even between brothers and sisters affection was rare. One by one, the gods had left the blood-soaked earth in disgust, until finally, last of all, Justice herself gave up trying to make her voice heard among humans, and fled, first to the mountains and then into the starry sky.[3] Ever since then, humans have been yearning for her return.

Tales of humankind's earlier, golden age and its bitter subsequent decline are told and told again in different times and places. And the longing to discover something more than we are living, which will restore a once existent harmony between the gods and their creation, seems to be an archetypal pattern, written into human nature. It has fuelled the great religions, and a continuing search for political justice. It is behind the myriad small Utopian communities that have sprung up over the centuries to challenge mainstream values, and informs the contemporary feminist myth of an age of matriarchal peace. And somewhere behind all these and more, is the lasting energy which the Greeks imaged as Themis, the deity of right order and natural and divine justice. Once, people travelled to Delphi to learn how the ways of humans could be brought into accord with those of the gods. Now, activists for the world's environment, or for fair trade, seek to bring the ways of humans into accord with those of nature before our own fallen world breaks down even further. Across the centuries, the psychological impulse behind these quests has been the same. Built into human beings, it seems, is a memory in the form of an image of the past, which is also a call to the future. In living on, the different collective stories of a Golden Age keep alive the idea and energy of new possibilities – for if something can be imagined, then it must already exist in potential.

These stories are about the interdependence of human energy and that of the cosmos. They tell that when people are in accord with 'the gods' or the complexities of their own true human nature, then the whole natural world is also in balance. At a time when the dis-ease of so many individuals seems to echo the disruptions that humans themselves have brought to the natural world, that perception may seem the more important. This understanding of interdependence seems universal, across time and space. In ancient Chinese philosophy, it is the state of Tao, and in Chapter 4 the story of the rainmaker illustrated how, in this state, individual harmony accords with that of nature itself. Hinduism expresses the same concept as *rta*, the pre-existent order or truth, and dharma, its manifestation in the lives of societies and individuals. Just as in the Greek Golden Age men and gods lived together in the bounty of nature, an ancient Sumerian epic recalls the time when the peaceful world was free of savage and dangerous beasts, 'when the whole universe, the people in unison' gave praise to their god Enlil. There was no discord between God and his creation in the Judeo-Christian Garden of Eden when he walked alongside his first-created humans in the cool of the evening. In those days of harmony between gods and humans, humans and nature, laws were redundant. In the Hindu epic, for instance, the return of the god-king Rama to his kingdom Ayodhya ushered in the Rama-Raja, the ideal rule under which there was no need to impose morality, because humans lived by the god's example. Plato understood something of the same: among virtuous men, he thought, there would be no need for laws.[4]

In today's world, such concepts may seem nothing but escapist fantasy. Indeed, much twentieth-century psychology has been concerned with relegating them to the nursery: current theories about human development have their own mythologies of the original and ideally blissful union between mother and infant, and these are taken not as reflection but as source of the great mythic traditions. The mythical world in which we now live is a dark and fallen one. Eve has long since eaten the apple to bring a consciousness that will wrest humans forever from the first harmony with God and nature. God has long cursed the ground on which humans tread, and condemned them to endless toil: 'In the sweat of your face/ you shall eat bread/ till you return to the ground, /for out of it you were taken; you are dust, / and to dust you shall return' (Genesis 3: 19). So the only harmony of humans with that once bountiful nature would from now on be in death. Hinduism tells a parallel story: in the great cycle of creation, Friday 18 February 3102 BC saw the beginning of Kali-Yuga, an age as dark as the Age of Iron was to the Greeks. Kali, black Time herself, means the worst of everything: it is the losing throw at dice, and has to do with strife and quarrels, battles and war. And for us humans, that is still the way it is, for Kali-Yuga lasts for 432,000 years.[5]

Yet the ancient concepts of a pre-existent and abiding 'right order' go far beyond positive and negative manifestations. Tao and *rta* encompass both in a deeper balance that underlies and maintains all life. Psychologically, Jung saw these concepts as expressions of libido and the life process itself, in individuals as in nature. He wrote of *rta*, for instance, as 'the path of our destiny and of the law of our being' manifested also in the processes of nature which remain always constant. For him, too, Tao was a representation of the Self, that psychological energy which unites and contains all opposites. And importantly, those opposites do not lose their own nature and qualities. 'Right order' does not mean bending to a single rigid pattern or 'reforming', but embraces natural difference. Tao, says Jung, 'takes all that is wild, without denaturing it and turning it into something higher.'[6]

In this holding of opposites, the idea of 'right order' and divine justice contains both the imagery of a world fallen from its original state of harmony between gods, humans and nature, and the promise of a new age. In the Hindu cycle, humans are waiting for the tenth and last incarnation of Lord Vishnu, Kalki on his white horse, who will destroy this world and re-create it anew. In the great messianic prophecies of Isaiah, it is precisely the restoration of that essential harmony between God, humans and the natural order that is foretold. When the Mighty God, Everlasting Father, Prince of Peace, is reborn, his rule will be one of justice and righteousness, over a world where wolf and lamb, lion and calf, cow and bear, and child and serpent live in harmony: 'They shall not hurt or destroy/ in all my holy mountain;/ for the earth shall be full of the/knowledge of the Lord /as the waters cover the sea' (Isaiah 9: 6–8, 11: 6–9). For Christians, the birth of the divine child could indeed seem to herald a new Golden Age. The seventeenth-century English poet John Milton heard this promised in the heavenly musical harmonies which greeted Christ's birth:

> Yea, Truth and Justice then
> Will down return to men
> Orbed in a rainbow.[7]

So the memory of divine justice and the yearning for her return to earth is kept alive.

But in an important sense, she never left. The Justice who fled first to the mountains and then to starry heaven was not, they say, Themis herself, but Dike, one of her three daughters by Zeus, sister to Eunomia (Good Order) and Eirene (Peace). This story encapsulates the distinction between divine and human justice – between the archetypal, timeless idea carried by Themis and its manifestation in human time and affairs. The second may waver and even disappear; the first is always there as part of the human psychological make-up. Contemporary Greek gives language to the perception: words with the root *dike* refer to the (human) apparatus and administration of justice, while

Themis is its personification. The first change with cultural norms, as does the perception of what is just and right; the second has remained steadfast through the centuries, a reminder to legislators and administrators of the source of their laws.

This distinction between Themis and Dike is both ancient and consistent. 'The people should fight for the law as if for their city-wall,' says the Greek philosopher Heraclitus, for instance. He adds, 'All human laws are nourished by one, which is divine.' The difference between human and archetypal levels is echoed some 16 centuries later by the scholar Natale Conti, who explained in his lastingly influential *Mythologie ou Explication des Fables* that in the Golden Age humans behaved justly because it was their nature; when Dike fled the earth at the end of that age, he says, she left behind laws and precepts for humans to follow.[8]

Psychologically, the distinction can be perceived at work in individuals just as much as in societies. 'Real moral problems,' thought Jung, 'all begin where the penal code leaves off.' He explored the difference between moralities which change in time and place and a deeper, inner authority in terms of the distinction between the moral and ethical aspects of conscience. For him, the first appeals to *mores* or customs; the second comes into action when these are not enough to settle a profound conflict of duties. Then, he said, something seems to come up from the unconscious to resolve the issue: 'The nature of the solution is in accord with the deepest foundations of the personality, as well as with its wholeness: it embraces conscious and unconscious and therefore transcends the ego.' This is the inclusive realm of the Self, for which the moralistic superego 'is only a substitute'.[9]

In his own exploration of conscience, the archetypal voice of the 'inner other', which constantly challenges us to go beyond the demands of ego, Jungian analyst Murray Stein has developed a similar theme. For him, conscience has both solar (or masculine) and lunar (or feminine) aspects. The first come filtered through the individual's experience of others in the family and the wider world, which teaches what is acceptable and expected behaviour – not far from Freud's notion of the superego, either benign or harshly punishing. Lunar conscience, on the other hand, 'will be conceived as the oracular voice of nature', an intuition of a cosmic order of which humans themselves are part. In its positive aspect, it fosters a sense of what is 'right' for an individual's own nature; in the moon's dark phase, it brings dis-ease, the eruption of symptoms and even a fear of madness. As Stein emphasizes, these two aspects of conscience, solar and lunar, are at work not just in individuals but in social organization. For us, this 'lunar' aspect has to do with Themis. The 'solar' is related to Dike, who, as Hesiod tells, reports to her father Zeus infringements of the human law.[10] Solar conscience, says Stein:

> is the source of law and the inner representative of a particular society's laws, while lunar conscience is the source of the perception of justice, a

deeper sense of right and wrong that does not depend upon or reflect the 'common law', that transcends the commonly received rules and regulations that govern a specific society ... Lunar conscience speaks for that which is commonly known and accepted as human, but known and accepted because it rises up from the common substrate of the deep psyche and forms a sort of collective moral common sense. Lunar conscience arises out of the archetypal patterns, those common human building blocks of the mind that constitute our human heritage as sentient beings.[11]

The inescapable interplay between Dike and Themis, laws human and laws divine, outer morality and inner ethical 'knowing', is imaged and recounted in legend and story, statue and canvas, from the early stories of Dike's flight to the multiplicity of nineteenth-century representations of Justice and beyond. The distinctions, as they interweave with social and political life, are sometimes clear and sometimes blurred. But by tracing them in the Western tradition, as this chapter now does, glimpses emerge both of the ways of Justice herself and of ways in which she has been used and even abused.

Through it all, and remarkably, the image of Justice has remained as a steadfast feminine presence in the very administration of patriarchal order. And from very early on, that presence carries echoes of more ancient and ample feminine powers. Dike becomes the maiden Astraea, who can still be seen in the night sky as the constellation Virgo, a reminder of the essential link between the heavenly and earthly orders. But alongside her starry aspect, she is still linked to the ancient power of Mother Earth, whose grandchild she is. She has also been seen to have affinities with Atargatis, the Syrian snake goddess and Heavenly Virgin of Carthage, who appeared so strikingly in Diana's drawings (Figures 2.1, p.27 and 2.2, p.28). As the scholar Frances Yates says: 'The just virgin is thus a complex character, fertile and barren at the same time; orderly and righteous, yet tinged with oriental moon-ecstasies.'[12]

From very early on, there was a yearning for the rediscovery of the old feminine energy. The Roman poet Virgil was one who thought the day had already come for Astraea's return. He saw fulfilment of the prophecy of the legendary wise woman, the Cumean Sibyl, whom we have already met in the last chapter. She had foretold a new Golden Age, ruled once more by Kronos, under his Roman name of Saturn. And now, says Virgil:

the last age of Cumae's prophecy has come;
The great succession of centuries is born afresh.
Now too returns the Virgin; Saturn's rule returns;
A new beginning now descends from heaven's height.
O chaste Lucina, look with blessing on the boy
Whose birth will end the iron age at last and raise
A golden through the world: now your Apollo rules.[13]

Some say the child hailed by Virgil in his fourth *Eclogue* was the one to be born to Octavia, the sister of the Emperor Augustus, and the poem created as homage to him. But for Constantine, the first Christian Emperor, it was not the coming of the golden Augustinian Age which Virgil was heralding, but the birth of Christ himself. When Constantine asks 'Who is the Virgin who returns?' he is thinking not of Justice, but of Christ's mother, the Virgin Mary. St Augustine also took the Cumean prophecy as messianic and the tradition became woven into medieval Christian belief.[14]

Legends interweave, stories and traditions intertwine, and the names of Justice sometimes become interchangeable. Yet underneath them all, bringing them all together, is not the changing nature of human justice, but something beyond. When the fifteenth-century philosopher Marsilio Ficino hymns Justice as 'salvation of mankind, Queen of the world', it is *themis* energy that he evokes, the divine and natural law which orders the universe:

> That divine law, by which the universe abides and is governed, kindles in our minds at their creation the inextiguishable light of natural law, by which good and evil are tested. From this natural law, which is a spark of the divine, the written law arises like a ray from that spark. . . .
>
> Oh eternal bonds of the human race! Most wholesome cure for our sickness! Common soul of society! Justice that is blissful life! Justice that is heavenly life! Mother and Queen of the golden age, sublime Astraea, seated among the starry thrones! Goddess, we beg you, do not abandon your earthly abode, lest we miserably sink into the iron age. Heavenly goddess, we beseech you, live ever in human minds, that is, in citizens who belong to the heavenly country, so that for the present we may imitate the divine life as well as we can, and that in the time to come we may live it to the full.[15]

Far from forsaking her earthly abode, as time went on Justice could increasingly seem to have returned to it full time, as monarchs sought to portray themselves, and be portrayed, as her very embodiment. The identification of Queen Elizabeth I of England with Justice, for instance, was very deliberate: she *was* Astraea. From the start of her reign, this Virgin Queen was adorned with the symbolism of Justice, Purity and Peace. Legends came together when Protestant theologians, in their opposition to Catholicism, deliberately compared her with and even lauded her over the Virgin Mary, whose return Constantine had seen prophesied so many centuries earlier. When Sir John Davies of Hereford asked in his *Hymns to Astraea* 'But whereto shall we bend our lays?' he already knew the answer:

> Even up to Heaven, again to raise
> The Maid, which thence descended;
> Hath brought again the golden days,
> And the entire world amended.

There are 26 of these hymns, and the first letters of each line of each of them spell out ELISABETHA REGINA 26 times.[16]

By then, the distinction between the source of Justice and her manifestation in human affairs had long been blurred. Already in Roman times, when Dike became the goddess Justitia, her image appeared on coins – and so reminded people of the value of her energy to the state. This civic role would remain a central one, as Justice, now no longer a deity, became the greatest of the four great classical Virtues. Cicero placed her over Prudence, Temperance and Fortitude as their 'mistress and queen', and when the quarternity became the cardinal virtues of Christianity, those on which all others hinged (from the Latin *cardo*, a hinge), Justice remained pre-eminent.

At the start of the fifteenth century, Christine de Pizan discovered that for herself when she set out to write *The Book of the City of Ladies*. This city was designed to house the great women of history and legend whose achievements had been discounted by men for so long, and in her delightful work Christine was guided from start to finish by avatars of the three Fates of antiquity, now known as Dame Reason, Dame Rectitude and Dame Justice. All of them helped her build her city and introduced her to the many extra-ordinary women who would populate it. But Dame Justice was the one who completed it, by putting on the roofs, adding the inns and hotels for its inhabitants, and introducing the city's Queen, who was also the Queen of Heaven. As Dame Justice rather briskly explained: 'I could give a rather long account of the duties of my office. But, put briefly, I have a special place among the Virtues, for they are all based on me.' More than 100 years later, Queen Elizabeth of England's own special place would be demonstrated when she was portrayed in front of a pillar on which the three theological virtues (Faith, Hope and Charity) as well as the four cardinal ones were displayed. Justice takes the central position, and she seems to be wearing the same dress as the queen.[17]

The Book of the City of Ladies had its first (and until 1981 its only!) translation into English in 1521. But by then there was a growing wealth of allegorical imagery across Europe, which was to accumulate until well into the nineteenth century. Figures of the Virtues appeared in statuary and on stained glass, in public buildings and even, as time went by, on posters. And the more they proliferated, the heavier, more lifeless and less imaginative their images generally became, as if weighed down by their identification with the state and the burdens of public office imposed on them. Yet Justice inexhaust-ibly retained her special place at the heart of public administration, and presides to this day over law courts and other public buildings – from London's central criminal court at the Old Bailey to New York's City Hall, from Mumbai's High Court of Justice to countless others across the world. And of all the virtues, she remains the best known. Few people nowadays, perhaps, would be able to identify Prudence, Temperance or Fortitude. But Justice is instantly recognizable by her scales, her sword and her blindfold.

These accessories tell their own symbolic tales. Christine de Pizan's Dame Justice would have recognized the scales, for her own emblem of a golden measure served the same purpose: to give to each supplicant their rightful portion, no more nor less. But the scales also link Justice to a far more ancient goddess, with whom Themis has much in common – Egyptian Maat, the embodiment of Truth and the right ordering of the universe. Without her, life itself was impossible, for she was food and drink to the sun-god Re: she personified the basic universal laws. Her name means 'straight'; 'maat' is also the rule that craftsmen use to keep their lines true, as well as the rule of law that keeps humans 'straight'. Maat knew the supreme value of the blood-soul: it was the *heart* of each person who died which was weighed on her scales against her Feather of Truth, to see whether they were fit to enter the world beyond.[18]

Justice's sword would be recognized too, by the many Christian saints, male and female, who wielded their own to defend the right. In medieval Christian iconography, the Archangel Michael, both a weigher of souls and another slayer of the dragon-serpent of evil, pre-empted the combination of scales and sword. But through today's psychological lens, these attributes still carry something of Themis's energy. The scales give an image of her capacity to hold opposites in balance. The sword represents the discrimination that discerns and maintains 'right order', double-edged to symbolize the unitary power of creation and destruction, life and death, which once belonged to the ancient Triple Goddess. United in the hands of Justice, the scales and sword give an image of both holding together and splitting apart, the two great actions which maintain nature itself. In many times and places, these movements have been identified as attributes of 'the feminine' and 'the masculine', each with their essential part to play in the sustaining of life. So when masculine and feminine are held in equal honour, it could be said, then there is Justice.

By the early seventeenth century, when the popular iconographer Cesar Ripa brought out his *Iconologia*, scales and sword were standard attributes of Justice. But he found others as well – including a dog at Justice's feet and a snake entwining under her sword-hand. For Ripa, these two unlikely companions are stern allegorical reminders that 'inflexible Justice bows neither to friendship nor hatred'.[19] But in the image of the snake, there is also a more subtle reference, an energy-memory of Themis and her guardian Python, and of Atargatis, the Syrian snake-goddess whose imagery became entwined with that of Dike/Astraea. This reminder of the ancient order remains insistent. One of the most popular reproductions of Justice in the United States, the one lawyers can buy for their desks and even on table lamps, is based on a nineteenth-century bronze called Themis (Figure 6.3).

As Figure 6.3 shows her, the blindfold goddess carries the expected scales and sword. But at her feet, even entwining around them, is a large, coiled snake. In Christian iconography, it is not uncommon for saints to be

Figure 6.3 Themis and the serpent remain entwined (N. Mayer). Used by permission of *For Counsel Inc., the Catalog for Lawyers.*

portrayed as trampling the serpent of evil underfoot. But here the goddess seems not at all perturbed by her companion as she seems rather to rest her foot on its neck. They seem to go together to make the image whole: this snake, perhaps, is more to be honoured as a reminder of Themis's ancient protector Python than to be destroyed.

There is nothing ancient, however, about Justice's blindfold, which seems to have become standard during the sixteenth century. Ripa is clear about its purpose: 'She is blindfolded, for nothing but pure reason, not the often misleading evidence of the senses, should be used in making judgements.' The ideal of the impartiality of the law, of justice as blind to differences between opposing parties and applying only an objective, abstract standard, is one that every Western law student learns to this day. Importantly, however, the ideal draws on a concept of a source of righteousness and truth that is somehow pre-existent and inherent. The saviour foretold by Isaiah had this quality: 'He shall not judge by what his eyes see/or decide by what his ears hear;/ but with righteousness he shall judge the poor, / and decide with equity for the meek of the earth' (Isaiah 11: 3). Christine de Pizan's Dame Justice also drew 'straight' from this source: 'I do not bend anywhere,' she says, 'for 1 have not friend nor enemy nor changeable will: pity cannot persuade me nor cruelty move me. My duty is only to judge, to decide, and to dispense according to each man's just deserts.' And in a self-definition that carries very exactly the energy of Themis, she adds: 'I sustain all things in their condition, nothing could be stable without me.'[20]

Dame Justice needed no blindfold, however, to ensure she carried out her duty. So why has it been so widely used? The imagery it conjures is by no means always positive. The blindfolded may be guarded from using what they see to feed the personal prejudice that would skew their judgement. But they may also be blinded to the truth before them: medieval images of Synagogia, for instance, were often represented with a blindfold, to indicate that the Jews had not seen the truth of Christianity. In romantic images across the years, cupids and even Eros himself are often seen blindfolded too, to indicate the follies and confusions of judgement wrought by love.[21] So what is Justice failing to see? And, in another association to the image, another question: who has captured Justice, blindfolded her and even threatened her with execution, like a prisoner before a firing squad?

The blindfold first appeared at a time of great cultural change. The age-old order of the universe, obedient to God's laws, was being challenged: Copernicus, Kepler and Galileo were pioneering the scientific age in which reason would triumph and de-sacralized matter would become the object of its study. The Christian church, upholder of the old order, was itself in bitter schism, and brutally projecting its own confusions and hatreds: from the fifteenth to the seventeenth centuries, in Europe and New England too, churches were seized by the appalling cruelties of the witch-craze, in which women in particular suffered persecution for their supposed association with the Devil. The *Malleus Maleficarum*, the late fifteenth century Dominican manual for finding and destroying witches, even identifies those 'in or by whom the devil either speaks or performs some astonishing operation' as *Pythons*, so associating the Delphic snake energies with witches, and further distancing the oracular voice of the blood-soul from the world of reason.[22] At the same time, the power of collective beliefs was being irrevocably weakened with the rise of individual consciousness and its glorious artistic expression. Secular institutions were developing: monarchs might still be portrayed as the personification of Justice, but the courts were becoming increasingly separated from unchallengeable, quasi-divine regal authority.

Justice was blindfolded, then, at a time of great cultural change and rapid development in Western consciousness. Perhaps Justice's blindfold signalled that judges were becoming more independent and impartial, less quick to respond to regal whim. Or perhaps now that the apparatus of law was losing its protective monarchical mystique, its human fallibilities, limitations and downright cruelties were becoming more apparent: Justice no longer seemed all-seeing. Perhaps too, however, the growing separation of blood-soul and spirit-soul, and denigration of the wisdom of the first in favour of the under-standings of the second, meant that the divine 'natural justice of Themis herself was indeed being captured and subjected to human laws. In his explanation for the blindfold, Cesare Ripa was explicit: it was to signal that justice should depend on reason alone and not the evidence of the senses. So the language and wisdom of the blood-soul must be ruthlessly excised. Albrecht Durer seems to understand what is being lost by this, in a woodcut from the end of the fifteenth century. In Figure 6.4 he portrays Justice, sword in hand, scales at her feet, being blindfolded by a fool.

This growing antagonism to the laws of the blood-soul, together with the development of individual Western consciousness out of collective assump-tions, also brought an end to unquestioning acceptance of human laws as a reflection of divine will. The further those laws were removed from *themis* consciousness, it seems, the more it became apparent that their implacable refusal to be swayed by individual circumstance, so grimly expressed by Christine de Pizan's Dame Justice, could bring its own terrible harshness. In the mid-sixteenth century, Pieter Breugel produced a shocking illustration of just this perception. Figure 6.5 shows Justice wielding her sword and protected by a posse of soldiers, blind to the beheading, hangings and terrible tortures being carried out all around her. As Dame Justice had said, 'Pity can-not persuade me nor cruelty move me.' Now perhaps people were increasingly asking: Why not?

At the same time, Breugel's vision brings a reminder of another, darker side of the natural and divine order that was imaged in Themis. Nature is both benign and terrible in her total disregard for individual life and circum-stance, and so may be the deities who personify her manifold nature. When Themis's divine law is flouted, when the wisdom of the blood-soul is denied, then there is an inescapable price to pay. Then the goddess's dark counterpart Nemesis will appear – implacable, relentless and bearing divine vengeance on her wings. The double-edged sword of Justice, which may bring both destruc-tion and creative discrimination, is a reminder of the dual nature of the once-great goddess, as both bringer and taker of life. This dual nature of divine power has exercised sages through the ages. In one expression of it, an old Jewish teaching has God seated with justice at his left hand, but love and mercy at his right; with the left he dashes to pieces, with the right, he is glorious to save.[23] The understanding that the world cannot survive on the basis of justice alone had long ago been expressed by the Psalmist. Praising God's favour towards his people, he sang that 'Mercy and truth are met

Figure 6.4 Who blindfolded Justice? (Albrecht Durer). Beinecke Rare Book and Manuscript Library, Yale University.

together; righteousness *(justitia)* and peace have kissed each other.' And in an echo of Themis as the oracular power of earth, he continues: 'Truth *shall spring out of the earth*; and righteousness shall look down from heaven' (Psalm 85, italic added).

Many medieval writers drew on this vision of heaven and earth reuniting under divine order in their own meditations on God's justice and redemption, and exploration of God as both harsh and loving. In an early fifteenth century French morality play, for instance, humankind is on trial before God's judgement seat. This time, Justice stood at his right hand, advocating against Mercy, Truth, Charity and Wisdom who were on the side of humankind; only through Christ's passion and intervention, says the script, can the five be reconciled. The recognition that Justice needs to be tempered with Mercy was enduring. When the British built the huge neo-Gothic law court of Mumbai at the end of the nineteenth century, both Virtues were enthroned atop its 120-foot towers.[24] They remain there still.

SCOPVS LEGIS EST AVT VT EV QVE PVNIT EMENDET, AVT POENA
EIVS CAETEROS MELIORES REDDET AVT SVBLATIS MALIS CAETERI SECVRIORES VIVAT.

Figure 6.5 The vision of Justice is destroyed (Pieter Breugel). Courtesy of Bibliothèque
Royale de Belgique, Bruxelles – SII 135128.

The struggle to bring the apparatus of justice back to its underlying divine
and natural origins remains a persistent theme. Somewhere encoded in
human beings, it seems, there is a 'knowledge' that particular judicial systems
are informed and supported by a 'natural law' or 'right order' which is timeless and universal, and that to ignore that is to invite Justice's wrath. However
much that underlying structure of 'natural law' may be ignored, flouted and
denigrated in practice, the knowledge remains that Dike, or human justice,
owes her life to her mother Themis.

And however much human justice turned from the promptings of the
blood-soul to the call of reason, from the 'feminine' virtues to the 'masculine'
ones, the image of the former is always there. Right from their first appear-
ances, all the Virtues – Faith, Hope and Charity, Justice, Prudence, Temperance and Fortitude – have been not just feminine in grammatical gender but
represented in female form. This has always caused headaches for theologians
raised in the dominant Judeo-Christian belief that women are by their very
nature inferior to men. Back in the first century CE, Philo Judeus had been
puzzling his way out of the conundrum by explaining that as god was masculine, anyone in second place to him would be represented as feminine: 'For
pre-eminence always pertains to the masculine, and the feminine always

comes short and is lesser than it.' By the seventeenth century, Cesare Ripa was explaining that representing a Virtue as a woman did three things: it followed grammar, expressed through the (superior) beauty of woman the Platonist idea that beauty in all its forms reflects the divine, and emphasized, because human women are weaker, the extraordinary nature of Virtue.[25]

Psychologically, however, the lasting presence of female figures in the male strongholds of administration, the law and public affairs has had a compensatory value. It has served as a reminder of the distant origin of the 'rule of law', and kept alive at least an image of balance between masculine and feminine energies in these places of power and influence. This may seem grossly at odds with the facts of male and female representation in their corridors, at least until fairly recently, and with some lastingly influential attitudes too about women's unsuitability for this 'male world'. As time went on, the new depth psychology would add its weight to the old judgements. Freud, for instance, in his own version of the ancient Aristotelian theory of the deficiency of women, thought that women were by their nature lacking in a sense of justice. This, he said, was because of the large part played by envy in their mental life. 'The demands of justice,' he thought, 'are a modification of envy: they lay down the conditions under which one is willing to part with it.' For women, however, this relinquishment was not possible: their envy, stemming as it did from their lack of a penis, was inescapably built into them.[26]

Yet what the images of Justice and other Virtues point to is another way of perceiving, in which 'masculine' and 'feminine' are unhooked from actual men and women to widen our understanding of the energy at work. Then it becomes possible to ask, for instance, whether there is any difference between 'masculine' and 'feminine' approaches to justice. There is some evidence that there may be. In her early studies of moral decision making, Harvard psychologist Carol Gilligan found that men tend to operate from abstract standards such as 'truth', 'equality' and 'fairness' which should be applicable in any context, and which in theory underpin the administration of the law. Women, however, tend to work from a sense of relationship in particular situations, giving particular priority to minimizing hurt to others. These distinctions are not absolute: as Gilligan emphasizes, they represent two approaches rather than a generalization about either sex. But they do suggest distinctive masculine and feminine perceptions of justice – one that discriminates right and wrong according to unyielding principles, another which works towards reconciliation of conflicting interests with the minimum of harm.[27] In the terms of this book, these contrasting ethics represent the distinctly different languages of the spirit-soul and the blood-soul. They are a reminder that alongside and below the realm of Dike, that of the law and morality, lies the realm of Themis, the deep ethic which seeks to bring together disparate energies in her own 'right order'.

How is humankind living with these two aspects? Even if Justice is blindfolded, she is not blind. If the blindfold were removed, what would Justice see and reveal through her vision? There might be some shocks. At the end of the nineteenth century, the Austrian Ministry of Culture commissioned the artist Gustav Klimt to make three ceiling paintings for the ceremonial hall of the new university, representing Philosophy, Medicine and Jurisprudence under the general theme of the 'triumph of light over darkness'. Klimt turned this bland municipal contract on its head and what he produced was so shocking that it was never hung. In Jurisprudence, the triple goddess is illumined in the high distance; her epiphanies as Truth, Justice and Law look down impassively on a pot-bellied, broken old man held in the grip of a great octopus whose sinuous shapes are echoed in the coiling of three other, no less impassive, female figures.[28]

Is this what humankind has made of Themis's energy? Is the great primeval power that lies behind the sturdy, even stodgy, allegorical imagery of the Virtues, showing here a terrifying aspect because it has not been honoured enough? And what would a rehonouring be like? The next chapter finds a hint of an answer, exploring one way in which legal institutions are currently trying to reconnect to Themis's own deep justice.

Chapter 7

Restoring *themis* energy

All over the West, and wherever its institutions have taken hold, people come together in the name of Justice to seek her ways. Yet what emerges from the criminal lawyers' offices and courtroom corridors can be very far from the goddess's own deep order. Victims whose sense of control in their own lives has been fearfully shattered can be made to feel yet more helpless by a legal system in which professionals speak for them and their own voice is circumscribed. Offenders are even less heard and remain mute targets of fear and hate, often locked in denial of the significance of their actions. The families and friends of both victims and offenders seldom have any role. And the overall result of the lengthy, expensive and painful legal process is often only a shallow restoration of individual and social order. Victims may feel a respite of relief, but no deeper sense of safety than before. In many places, more and more people are sentenced to harsher and harsher conditions in already overflowing prisons which too often teach them little except bitterness and new ways of offending. In England and Wales, for instance, no fewer than three-quarters of new crimes are committed by people who have already been convicted of others.

So far from bringing transformation, the administration of justice can often reinforce the fear, misunderstanding and hatred between 'them', the offenders, and 'us', the law-abiding majority. For all their efforts to maintain and restore 'right order' by punishing and banishing their wrongdoers, societies and communities are often made no more whole than they were. They may even become more divided. As Lawrence Sherman, professor of criminology at Cambridge University, summarizes it:

> The classic mistaken assumption of conventional justice is to punish offenders as if they will never come back from prison to live among us. But with rare exceptions, they all come back. When they do, we depend on them not to cause more harm in the community. We are all interdependent in a shrinking world: criminals, victims and the wider society. High rates of reconviction suggest that we are not doing what is needed to support their interdependence.[1]

The psychological assumptions underlying conventional justice are deep-seated. Themis herself once saw their dangers and an old story, of how a single attempt at keeping out dissent escalated into a tragically destructive decade of war, is still psychologically relevant today. The trouble began at the marriage of the sea-nymph Thetis and the hero Peleus – a sumptuous affair, and cause of great rejoicing. All the Olympians were there, bidden by Themis, their golden thrones especially imported for the occasion. All, that is, except one: nobody had invited Eris, nobody wanted Strife at the wedding. And why should they? She is a real creature of darkness, this fatherless daughter of dreadful Night, and herself the mother of Famine and Pains, Murders, Battles and Fights, Lawlessness and Ruin. But like the bad fairy whom nobody invites to the Sleeping Beauty's christening, she cannot be ignored, and any attempt to shut her out will just make her angrier and more destructive. 'Once she begins she cannot stop,' as Homer says. 'At first she seems a little thing, but before long, though her feet are still on the ground, she has struck high heaven with her head.' Not that on this occasion she needed to go so far; she was far craftier than that. All she did was to roll a golden apple innocently labelled 'For the Fairest' at the feet of the goddesses Hera, Athene and Aphrodite. And out of their rivalry for the prize, the whole bloody conflict of the Trojan War unrolled, and with it the terrible sufferings that beset not just the decade of fighting but generations to come.[2]

This story carries still relevant psychological truths, which seem to hold good for societies as much as individuals. What it tells is that if the elements that make for Strife are repressed or denied, they will intensify in their efforts to come to psychological consciousness and be acknowledged. As Diana discovered, it was her attempts to keep imprisoned her own Titanic emotions that led her to so much distress. Once she could accept these shadow aspects as an inescapable part of her own psychological reality, they could become creative and lead her to a fuller sense of herself – not more 'perfect' but more whole. As Jung put it, 'One does not become enlightened by imagining figures of light, but by making the darkness conscious.'[3]

The same psychological law applies in communities and societies. When they deny their psychological shadow to preserve their own good opinion of themselves, then the way to the escalation of strife is wide open. First, that shadow is projected on to others – the 'irresponsible', the 'underclass', the 'criminals', the 'foreigners', the 'outsiders', the 'evil empire' – the enemy without and within which is to be hunted down, punished and even destroyed. Then when those who carry the shadow retaliate in an attempt to be heard – when criminals, for instance, reoffend – the original projection is simply reinforced and the escalation begins again. Once more it becomes essential for 'us' to preserve a sort of unity and illusion of safety by redoubling efforts to separate from the 'them' who carry all that is fearful and despised. To break this cycle by acknowledging 'our' shadow and withdrawing the projections is hard psychological work, for that shadow is by definition everything that 'we' have no wish to be. There is no simple technique: Jung thought the process was more like one of diplomacy, demanding long and difficult negotiations.

> The suffering shows the degree to which we are intolerable to ourselves. 'Agree with thine enemy', outside and inside! That's the problem! I admit it is not easy to find the right formula, yet if you find it you have made a whole of yourself, and that, I think is the meaning of human life.[4]

What seems true for individuals also applies to collective relationships between them: the humbling work of shadow reclamation also brings the hope of a more whole society. Already in the old stories there is the hint of this possibility of transformation. Hesiod, for instance, writes of two Strifes – the cruel one who makes battles and war, and the other, 'set in the earth, an aid to men', who encourages tough but necessary competition and keeps people from becoming lazy.[5]

So what could happen if Strife were acknowledged, and invited into the places and processes of justice? At the moment, her place there is strictly regulated by the time-honoured formalities of the adversarial system. But this leaves out the raw and painful emotions of all those involved, whether victim, offender, or representative of the community to which they both belong. If these emotions were acknowledged and worked with, could some of Themis's deep natural order and divine justice be restored?

The idea may seem far from the realities of police and probation, court and cell. But for the last 30 years or so, the practice of restorative justice has been trying to translate it into action. In New Zealand and Australia, across Europe and North America, different restorative justice schemes have been gathering strength to become 'one of the most important developments in contemporary crime policy – a vibrant international campaign'. Many deal with youth justice and less serious offences, but by no means all: it seems, in fact, that this approach is more effective when applied to the graver crimes. Research is also showing that restorative justice actually leads societies towards their own 'right order'. In one authoritative study of many different schemes, at least twice as many offences were brought to justice than through conventional legal systems. The approach brings its own healing, as both victims and offenders report deeper satisfaction with its outcomes: victims feel less burdened by the psychological effects of the crime and less desire for revenge; and reoffending rates are often dramatically lower than under conventional systems. By the turn of the twenty-first century, the idea had taken root enough for the United Nations to make a statement of 'Basic Principles on the Use of Restorative Justice': this began by saying that it should be introduced at all stages of criminal justice procedure.[6]

The first thoroughgoing incorporation of the approach was in New Zealand, as a response to the disproportionately high number of Maori people in prison and the desire of Maori elders to take care of their own, as they largely had up until the 1940s. The 'family group conference', introduced in a youth and family justice act of 1989, has been widely influential since. As well as leading a way forward, the act also looks back, to bridge past and future: the family group conference was modelled on the traditional Maori justice of the *marae* or community centre, itself fuelled by the spiritual energy of Papatuanuku, or Earthmother.[7]

How does this deep energy inform the processes of justice? Here is just one story. Four boys broke into a school, got drunk, and accidentally set the place on fire. Instead of being arrested and charged, they were brought to a three-day family group conference. On the first day, teachers and parents tried to make the youths realize just what harm and disruption their action had caused. But they sat there quite unmoved. Then on the next day, a young girl sat herself in front of them with a scrapbook she had kept in her classroom. She told them that this half-burned, half-charred book of family photos was all she had left as a memento of her brother, who had died about a year earlier. And at that point, the tears started to trickle down the boys' faces. It seemed that the young girl had arrived at just the right moment. It was a turning point. Gradually the boys owned their offence, apologized to everyone affected by it and gave up their weekends to help build a new playground. Instead of being punished and stigmatized as bad lads, they became something like local heroes. And that was the last time they came to police attention.[8]

The schemes vary from country to country and area to area, from sentencing circles in different parts of North America to community conferences both there and across Australia and New Zealand, from victim–offender mediation schemes in Europe to English restorative cautioning and Norwegian neighbourhood boards. But essentially, each draws on the same principles and the same moral vision – a vision of what Sherman describes as 'redemption through acknowledgement of responsibility for having caused harm'. It is just this acknowledgement, as he points out, that conventional justice systems fail to encourage, leaving offenders able to deny that they have in any way acted immorally. His 'defiance theory' posits that restorative justice, by engaging people who have committed a crime in a moral discussion about whether crime is wrong, can lead them to redefine themselves as law-abiders and so to conclude that what they did was wrong and should not be repeated. So restorative justice turns not to punishment, but to a theory of obeying the law by persuasion, which is the ultimate commitment to the rule of law.[9]

The principles underlying restorative justice reach down to ancient roots in this search for 'right order'. The very words associated with the approach – restore, repair – suggest that something lost is being refound and re-established. Its advocates have reached into the historical past to suggest that before the rise of state power in the twelfth century, the basis of all European justice was not retribution but restoration. Far from being a free-for-all of private vengeance in which the strong crushed the weak, they say, justice was then contained within a system of ritual and symbol, and its object was to hold people together in community. As the historian Harold Burman says, the old law was based on:

> a sense of the wholeness of life, of the interrelatedness of law and all the other aspects of life, a sense that legal institutions and legal processes as well as legal norms and legal decisions are all integrated in the harmony of the universe. Law, like art and myth and religion, and like language itself, was for the peoples of Europe . . . not primarily a matter of making and applying rules in order to determine guilt and fix judgement, not an institution to separate people from one another on the basis of a set of principles, but rather a matter of holding people together, a matter of reconciliation.[10]

This is the realm of Themis's divine and natural law, the goddess's own 'right order'. European justice and other systems based on it have long lost this sense. But traditional societies have not. From the start, concepts of restorative justice have drawn on the inspiration of some ancient wisdoms – not just those of the Maori people but others as well. In Canada, for instance, a Crown Attorney recalls meeting with a Cree First Nation chief, his young council and some community elders. He asked them what they used to do to those who misbehaved before the visiting courts came. One old woman said immediately, as if surprised that such a question could even be asked, 'We didn't do anything *to* them – we counselled them!' The visitor was sceptical, until he learned just how widespread this approach to wrongdoers was. A new approach to justice began when he was met in a remote community by a self-appointed 'police committee' of six men and six women, who had already been working with the offenders on his court list and their families as well. They had already decided a programme of education for them far more sensitively geared to their needs than anything 'official' justice could have produced.[11]

Importantly, the emphasis in indigenous justice systems is not on the exclusion of offenders, but on their reintegration. In the Navajo tradition of peacemaking, for instance, a wronged individual, helped where necessary by relatives and an official 'peacemaker', faces the perpetrator in a community meeting which is begun with a prayer. The wronged person makes a demand for restitution, but as Navajo concepts of freedom and individuality insist that one person cannot impose a decision on another, the perpetrator of the wrong must agree to make things right. The mediated discussion draws on the ancient case law – the stories of First Man and First Woman, the foolishness of Coyote and the wisdom of Horned Toad – to reach a just settlement. The cement of the whole process is the concept of *k'e*, which describes the proper relationship of people to each other, and enforces a binding judgement without resort to sheriff or jail.[12]

This community peacemaking approach is shared by many indigenous peoples, as researchers have found in South America and Africa; it has been suggested that the model was once universal. Now this ancient model is becoming influential again. (As a President of the American Bar Association once wrote: 'Our Navajo peers could teach us a thing or two about conflict resolution.') This is not without problems, not least for indigenous people who feel that their desire for a separate justice system has been hijacked by the state. Critics of restorative justice accuse its advocates of romanticizing and oversimplifying the complexities of and differences between traditional approaches to fit their own ideas of what ought to happen. They question the relevance of these models: these were justice systems, they say, designed for rural societies which no longer exist, in which the needs of the individual were subservient to those of the community and both were contained in belief systems unquestioned by either. Those beliefs, they point out, could sanction far harsher punishments than would many modern Western courts, including death and banishment. Some practices, like 'spearing' the thigh, still practised among Australian aboriginal peoples as symbolic reparation, would not be recognized outside their own societies. At the same time, critics say, some offences are treated far more leniently in traditional patriarchal communities than they are under Western law: many women do not at all feel protected by the legal system of their culture.[13]

Yet alongside and below these realities, the very many attempts to learn from indigenous justice models speak to the strength and depth of a seemingly universal yearning for social healing. This yearning is fuelled by what this book calls *themis* energy, which brings together different psychic forces and makes it possible to work with them. As the last chapter explored, the same yearning and energy are behind the nostalgia for the Golden Age – and the processes of restorative justice draw on it too. In doing so, they tap deep into the blood-soul which is Themis's realm. As Matt Hakiaha, a member of the New Zealand parole board, has written: 'The processes of traditional, indigenous justice create a shift in the discourse from cognition or "head thinking" to affect or "heart feeling".'[14]

For a start, restorative justice sees crime as the violation not of a law or a rule, or of 'the state' that draws these up, but of a *person* by another person. From this it follows that resolution of the violation must lie between and within those people: offenders need to become aware of the harm they have caused and repair it, and those offended against need some restitution and assurance that the violation will not happen again. Although restorative justice schemes take many forms, it seems that face-to-face meetings are by far the most effective. So the crucial participants, all of whom have chosen to be there, are assembled: the victim, the perpetrator, often family and close friends of both, and representatives of the community to which all of them belong. They meet not in the formal space of the courtroom, removed in its language and procedures from everyday life, but are brought together informally in local halls or meeting rooms. Instead of being designated a place that indicates their status and role, they will likely sit in the equality and containment of a circle: this evokes the power of the mandala, the symbolic image which, as Diana so strikingly discovered, not only expresses order but creates it. Having the participants sit so close together could also allow their heart rhythms to affect each other in ways explored in Chapter 4: it could help create the possibility of a more resonant field. The intense emotional power of the meeting is contained by careful procedures, designed to create a setting that allows the best possible chance of all being heard. No one is allowed to be passive, no one is to be banished: all are essential to the process of not receiving but *creating* a justice that aims both to heal the past and help build a less divided future.

This search for healing is a long way from the usual preoccupations of establishing guilt and due punishment. And in the search, there is opportunity for Themis's energy – and her insight – to be restored. As Howard Zehr, credited with the first detailed formulation of restorative justice, has written: 'Blindfolded under the pretence of fairness, [justice] is frequently unable to see the experience of those impacted by crime. Restorative justice removes this blindfold, exposing the people – victims, offenders and community – to full view.'[15]

Tearing off the blindfold is no soft option, as some sceptics have claimed. People who have committed offences may agree fairly matter-of-factly to enter the process. They may bring a whole mixture of motives – agreement to a path of least resistance, a desire to get it all over more quickly than by going through the courts, a gamble that they may get off more lightly. They are certainly not expected to show remorse; as facilitators often say, the aim is not to screen for remorse, but to achieve it.[16] Whatever the motive, however, the face-to-face encounter between victims and perpetrators may be hugely painful, humiliating and shameful. Those who have committed the crime often say that serving time in prison would have been very much easier. Yet it is through processing the raw emotions of both victims and offenders that healing may come, in a way which conventional Western systems cannot offer. In recent years, those systems have considered victims of crime far more carefully: their voice is now heard in impact statements, they may have the right to be consulted about sentencing and to receive compensation from public funds. But whatever their official place in formal procedures, victims can still feel grievously unsupported. However much their official position is strengthened, their interests remain secondary to those of the wider public and 'the state'. This can mean, for instance, that the very person from whom a victim seeks compensation as a crucial step towards healing is in no position to make even symbolic reparation, because he or she is in prison.

Restorative justice systems offer something different. The victim's voice is often the first to be heard. They have the opportunity to communicate their anger and fear, to explain just how devastating the effects of the crime may have been, and to seek directly from the perpetrator both some sort of compensation, symbolic or actual, as well as answers to the painful and insistent 'Why?' And now, the perpetrators cannot avoid them, as they can in court. They have to hear, for instance, that it just is not true that their crime doesn't matter 'because the insurance will pay', or 'because they're rich'. They have to hear that the violation of their home or person may leave victims deeply shaken in self-confidence, with their trust in others and their close relationships in tatters. Perpetrators can no longer use the silence imposed on them by legal procedure to focus simply on their own feelings about the impending verdict. They have to engage with victims and to speak. Through this process, they may begin to *feel* the impact that their actions have had on others, to see them as human beings rather than objects to be exploited, stereotypes of an 'enemy', or simply inconvenient.

So the people who committed the offence may begin to feel remorse, and if they see the shame that their action has brought to their own family, they too may feel shame and the beginning of a desire to make restitution. At the same time, they also have the chance to tell their story, which conventional systems deny them. The other participants, including the victims, can hear something of what led the offenders to act as they did, and so begin to see their human-ity as well as their offence. And community representatives may begin to realize that this is not just a story about individuals, but also one that stems from the way social opportunities are offered and denied. They may begin to learn that 'criminals' are very often also 'victims' as well. In this process, as mutual shadow projections begin to dissolve, there is a movement among all the participants from head to heart, thinking to feeling. In the language of the blood-soul explored in Chapter 4, there may even be the beginnings of a deeper heart resonance, and so the precursor of a more inclusive community.

As the restorative justice movement has grown, so has the role of local communities: what was originally seen primarily as a matter between victim and offender now increasingly also involves not just family and friends but other local interests. Critics of restorative justice, as we have seen, often accuse its supporters of sentimental appealing to involved and supportive 'communities', when actually, they say, it is the very lack of community in modern Western cities that often contributes to crime. Yet restorative justice is at work in cities just as much as rural areas. In fact, one of the best established initiatives in the United States works in the second most violent inner city in the country. Drawing on five years of previous experience, the Baltimore Community Conferencing Center opened in 2000, with the vision that 'Communities and individuals in our society will recognise that they can safely and effectively resolve conflicts together.' Within its wide remit, it works as an alternative to the courts for juvenile non-violent and first–time felony offenders, and to ease the re-entry to their community of those who have spent time in prison.[17]

How might the process work? Here is an example from an Australian scheme. A mother and father met with two young men then in prison, who had taken part in a robbery that led to their son's death. The actual gunman refused to be there, but the mothers of the offenders and friends of the victim were also part of the conference. The mother of the victim began by speaking to the young men of her pain and hate. She told them of her loss, and her desire that they should never have a moment's peace. Her husband echoed her emotions.

The young men spoke next. They had little to say after hearing the enormity of pain that their actions had caused, but the grief and remorse on their faces was evident. One of them said that he knew nothing he said could ever convince them that he should not be hated and despised.

Next, the mothers of the offenders spoke. They seemed to be ripped apart – by love for their own children, and by pain and horror at what those children had done. One mother said in agony, 'I must have done something as a mother to have caused this.' The victim's mother then left her own world of pain, and in a remarkable moment, reached out and cried, 'Oh no! You mustn't blame yourself!'

From that moment, things began to shift. The victim's friend spoke, a mutual mourning seemed to evolve: for the lost hopes and lost lives, and the fact that their arrival at this point together, in this room, with so much suffering, would always remain incomprehensible.

Months later, some of the participants in that conference were interviewed. The nightmares of the victim's mother had stopped; it was not easy for her, but at least she felt she had some life again. And remarkably, the victim's father and one of the offenders were appearing as speakers to troubled young people in the juvenile justice system, to try to show them the consequences of crime. So this young man was making something meaningful out of his crime, and the remaining years he had to serve in prison.[18]

Not all restorative justice stories are as healing as this one. Here is one example, this time from England. A young woman had violently robbed an older one of her handbag, hitting her over the head so brutally that the wound needed 70 stitches. The victim had been left devastated; for seven months she had been unable to leave her home, far less return to work. When the two women met, together with a mediator and family members, the younger one spoke of how she had been using crack cocaine at the time of the robbery and needed money for her next hit; she had been so violent because the victim had clutched her handbag so tightly.

The older woman listened silently, without any expression. Her daughter explained how traumatized her mother had been, and how badly the many family members she supported through her work had been affected. The younger woman's grandmother spoke next. Looking directly at her granddaughter, she expressed her horror and asked how the young women would have felt if it had been her own grandmother who had been so brutally attacked.

The young woman broke into tears, and crossed the room to kneel in front of her victim to ask forgiveness. The older woman did not stir. The others discussed what might be done. They assumed that the young woman would be sent to prison, and the meeting agreed that she should get help for her drug addiction and attend an anger management course. She promised to behave, and become a better person.

The victim still did not move or speak. But at the end of the meeting, when everyone moved on to tea and biscuits, she suddenly said loudly 'Young woman, come here!' She took her attacker's hand, and began to pray that she would turn her life around. Again in tears, the young woman promised she would. For the victim, the meeting was restorative indeed. The very next day, she went out to buy a new handbag, and went back to work.

For the perpetrator, there no such positive outcome. This young woman, still only 21 years old, was a victim too: she had been sexually assaulted at the age of eight, and raped twice and assaulted once since then. Her life experience added devastation: she had already been arrested 28 times for offences that included four robberies. Now she was sentenced to five years in prison, but released after only two because of her good behaviour and time served before her sentence. Six weeks later, she was arrested for another robbery and returned to prison.[19]

For this young woman, the process was not enough to offer what she needed to make something different of her life. Restorative justice has been likened to a powerful drug which needs to be carefully tested on different conditions and illnesses before it is generally prescribed.[20] Yet overall, research is showing that people are more likely to keep the promises they make in restorative justice meetings than they are to comply with court orders. The way those promises are arrived at may, however, create its own questions. Some critics are concerned that victims have less protection than they would in a court of law, because part of the state's task is to enforce laws that may be unpopular with 'the community' and to ensure, as communities may not, that weaker members are not victimized by more powerful ones. Others are concerned that it is offenders who have less protection than the courts can offer, and that they are made more vulnerable to punitively idiosyncratic decisions. 'The community' is by no means synonymous with kindness or understanding, and sometimes the agreed acts of symbolic reparation can shock in their harshness. Where, for instance, is the healing when a violent man is made to stand while his abused wife spits in his face, a young offender is forced to wear a T-shirt branded 'I am a thief', or a probationer living in a halfway house is told to wear diapers outside his clothes because he's behaving like a cry-baby?[21]

Yet alongside these stories there are others. There is the man who wanted nothing more than that the young man who broke his truck window should pay up and then go to jail – until he learned about the young man's circumstances at the community conference and ended up giving time and money to help him become the first of his family to graduate from high school.

There are the battling neighbours, who between them had called the police something like 75 times in an escalation of violent antagonism that got to knife- and gun-point. They used their community conference for a screaming match, until one of the mothers burst into tears and said that someone would end up dead if they didn't stop right now – and so took the first step towards a lasting agreement.

There is the young man who readily admitted stealing and wrecking someone else's car, for which he would have expected a punitive sentence in the normal way – but whose victim was not going to let him off so lightly. She made sure he understood just what the loss of her car meant to the family in terms of inconvenience, and even danger when she couldn't take her chronically asthmatic daughter to hospital. The tough young man now really understood what he had done, and accepted giving up his own car to the family, which for him was far more serious among his peers than going to prison.[22]

Clearly restorative justice, no less than conventional systems, needs safeguards. But in his own careful assessment of whether it is compatible with the rule of law, Sherman concludes that there is no conflict. In fact, he suggests, by providing more opportunities for questions and answers, whether face to face or otherwise, restorative justice may make the law far more accessible, and so actually reinforce its rule.[23] Through thousands of individual acts of reconciliation, some for more serious crimes, some for less, different schemes for restorative justice are showing that there is another way to dealing with a variety of offences than reinforcing the gulf between victim and offender and offender and the community of which they both are a part. At one level, this can lead to sometimes dramatically lower reoffending rates and far higher compliance with restitution arrangements than the courts achieve. At another it can lead to deeper healing for victims and the chance for offenders to discover not just what they should not be doing, but what they should. And what the approach also shows is that it is precisely through attempting to work with all the painful conflicts of emotion and perspective which a crime engenders that stronger 'communities' can slowly be built.

This is not happening only through the criminal justice system, for the principles on which restorative justice is based can be used wherever there is a need for people who have been separated by hurt and conflict to come together. So there are many schemes in warring neighbourhoods, in schools to deal with bullying, and in prisons to enable people convicted of grievous crimes to work with their victims towards reparation. Each encounter can be seen as one small step towards a future that also looks back to Themis's deep social order and natural and divine justice.

Some people say that only a minority of victims and perpetrators will ever be touched by a system that depends on the agreement of both parties to participate. But that is to discount the cumulative effect that the many individual experiences and different small schemes may have on future understanding and expectations within and across communities and societies.

Advocates are suggesting that these now justify testing the feasibility of 'restorative communities', in which every stage of the criminal justice system, every civic organization and every governmental institution that deals with harms is based on restorative principles.[24] In fact, one extraordinary example of such an attempt already exists, made on so grand a scale that its implications have reverberated across the world. This is what the next chapter is about.

Chapter 8

The road to reconciliation

When the South African Truth and Reconciliation Commission (TRC) held its first public meetings in April 1996, no one knew what to expect. On the opening day, the hall was packed, mostly with black people, under a banner which proclaimed the commission as 'Healing Our Past'. The Chairman, Archbishop Desmond Tutu, shook hands with those who would testify and the relatives who came with them. He lit a candle in memory of all who had died in the country's past and a colleague read out a commemorative roll of honour. Everyone sang the hymn *Lisalis' idinga lakho* ('Let your will be done'), which had been sung too when Nelson Mandela, now the country's President, had first met his African National Congress colleagues on his release from 27 years in prison. There were prayers, and a general welcome. The first witness took the oath, was welcomed and invited to sit before she chose the language she wished to speak in.

As the week went by, and the stories of brutality and suffering unfolded, no one could remain unaffected. Witnesses and audiences wept. The commissioners could hardly restrain their own tears – and once, when Singqokwana Malgas broke down while trying to describe the torture he had undergone, the chairman himself put his head on the table and sobbed uncontrollably. All this was broadcast in the 11 official languages of the country. Over and over again, radio listeners heard the deep, anguished wail of Nomonde Calata, whose husband had been horribly murdered, as she told the commission that she didn't know where the security forces had taken him. For one journalist, that cry became the 'signature tune' of the commission's work. They heard this too: 'I was making tea in the police station. I heard a noise, 1 looked up . . . Then he fell . . . Someone fell from the upper floor past the window . . . I ran down . . . It was my child. . . . My grandchild, but 1 raised him.' In South Africa, where for 50 years black people had suffered the most cruel and brutally far-reaching institutionalized racism the modern world had yet seen, the testimony of an ordinary cleaning woman was the headline on the national one o'clock news.[1]

By the turn of the twenty-first century, there had been more than 20 Truth Commissions across the world, from Argentina and Chile to Rwanda,

Ethiopia and the Philippines. In the wake of the bloodiest century yet known, where 90 per cent of the estimated 22 million people dead in conflicts were civilians, these commissions had become a crucial tool in 'transitional justice' from repression to democracy. 'Coming to terms with the past,' as one commentator puts it, 'has emerged as the grand narrative of the late twentieth and early twenty-first centuries. Individuals and entire nations are seeking to overcome their traumatic legacies and move forward; the past in a sense needs to be "got over", and perhaps more importantly needs to be seen to be "got over".'[2]

Among all the traumatic legacies, the intensity of that left by South Africa's history and myth, belief and politics, stands out. Under the 1913 Land Act, black ownership was already limited to 13 per cent of the country; by 1990 around three-quarters of the land belonged to just 50,000 white farmers or companies in a country of 40 million people, a tenth of whom had been displaced from their homes. Between those dates, more than 300 apartheid laws had accrued to control, disadvantage and harass black South Africans from birth to death. This was indeed a land from which justice had fled, where Themis herself was battered and blindfolded. Apartheid was enforced with increasing brutality, and eventually the rule of law could be by-passed altogether: between 1960 and 1990, more than 80,000 opponents of apartheid were detained without trial, including more than 15,000 children. So hugely disparate was the experience of black, 'coloured' and white South Africans that, as one commentator says, 'The notion of fractured memory is given new meaning. Memory is not fractured here; rather it is splintered, rent apart, torn into a multitude of pieces.'[3] It was this grievously wounded memory that was the Truth and Reconciliation Commission's raw material. And just as the material was uniquely rent and wounded, so the commission was distinct among all the others across the world.

The Commission was charged to establish as complete as possible a picture of the causes, nature and extent of the gross human rights violations the country had suffered since 1960, and to make recommendations to ensure that they would never happen again. It had a unique and contentious power to grant individual amnesty to those who told the truth about their part in the violations and could show that these were carried out in pursuit of purely political aims. Unusually among truth commissions, its hearings were public, and every effort was made to ensure that they involved and were witnessed by as many people as possible. The commission's advertisements ('Truth Hurts, but Silence Kills') urged people to come forward. Over 18 months, there was huge media coverage of more than 70 public hearings of witness to gross violations of human rights, others about institutional violations in medicine, the law and the churches, and others again about applications for amnesty. When the South African Broadcasting Corporation stopped transmissions from the hearings in the country's 11 official languages because of lack of funds, there was an outcry, even among white South Africans. The broadcasts were reinstated. By the end of the process, over 21,000 testimonies had been submitted and over 7000 applications for amnesty had been made. As the main compilers of the commission's seven-volume report put it, this had been 'probably the biggest single human rights survey in the history of the world'.[4]

But this was very far from being simply a fact-finding mission, on however huge a scale. The concept of *reconciliation* was built into the commission's title, purpose and work. The discovery and telling of truth was held important not only to honour the suffering, but to weave a shared memory of what had happened in the past and so, as the banner above those first hearings emphasized, to heal that past by bringing people together. The familiar dictionary definitions of 'reconciliation' have to do with 'conversion from a state of hostility or distrust', and 'the promotion of goodwill by kind and considerate measures'. This process can be both an inner and an outer one, another expression of the *themis* energy at work in Diana and in the restorative justice movement. Individuals can discover and become *reconciled* to aspects of themselves and their past. Better able to live with the truth of their own natures and what has happened to them, they are then more free to continue their life's journey. Communities and societies can go through the same process. Older usages of the word 'reconciliation' give some ideas of what else may be involved. It has also meant 'confession', 'making atonement', and purification of sacred objects after desecration or pollution: all these meanings could be found in the commission's aims and aspirations.

These in turn were based on the bedrock of the new South African interim constitution which – miraculously it seemed – had enabled the transition to democracy in 1994 without the bloodbath that so many people feared was inevitable. Under its provisions, the constitution said, it was now possible to address the gross violations of human rights and the legacy of hatred, fear, guilt and revenge, and it laid down the spirit in which this should be done: '[T]here is a need for understanding but not for vengeance, a need for reparation but not for retaliation, a need for *ubuntu* but not for victimisation.' This approach was in turn written into the legislation which set up the commission, whose very title – the Promotion of National Unity and Reconciliation Act – told of its supremely sensitive, controversial and vital task. Some people called it 'the Mother of All Laws'.[5]

So the Commission can be seen as a powerful expression of the archetypal energy which brings together disparate and warring psychological states, contains them so that each can be articulated, acknowledged and honoured, and works to refind the healing 'right order' between them. This is what this book calls *themis* energy, which draws on the pre-existent natural order of Mother Earth. In South Africa, it has another name, written into the country's constitution: *ubuntu*.

Ubuntu means, in the words of the isiZulu and isiXhosa proverb, 'a person is a person because of, through, other people'. This simple statement has huge implications. As Anton Lembede, the founding president of the ANC Youth League has put it:

> [The African] regards the universe as one composite whole, an organic entity, progressively driving towards greater harmony and unity, whose individual parts exist merely as interdependent aspects of one whole, realising their fullest life in the corporate life where communal contentment is the absolute measure of values. His philosophy of life strives towards unity and aggregation, towards greater social responsibility.[6]

This does not just mean that people with *ubuntu* are generous, hospitable and caring towards each other. It means that they are these things because they know that their own humanity, their own well-being, is inextricably linked with that of others, whoever those others may be. For Desmond Tutu, a person with *ubuntu*:

> has a proper self-assurance that comes from knowing that he or she belongs in a greater whole and is diminished when others are humiliated or diminished, when others are tortured or oppressed, or treated as if they were less than who they are. . . . *Ubuntu* means that in a real sense even the supporters of apartheid were victims of the vicious system . . . The humanity of the perpetrator of apartheid's atrocities was caught up and bound up in that of his victim whether he liked it or not. In the process of dehumanising another, in inflicting untold harm and suffering, the perpetrator was inexorably being dehumanised as well.[7]

This perception is also found in the different traditional cultures whose philosophies, as we saw in the last chapter, have been so influential in contemporary approaches to restorative justice; the understanding of life as an indivisible whole may also once have been the foundation of a European law of reconciliation. Importantly, these perceptions leave room for the differences between people. A Xhosa saying describes *ubuntu* as being like the fingers of a hand – not one is like another, yet they function together as a whole. Over 2000 years ago, St Paul was writing to the Corinthians in just the same way, describing the society of Christians as made up, like a human body, of different parts and limbs. As he points out, there would be no hearing if every part of the body was an eye, no sense of smell if the body was made up only of ears. Each part has its own function and all are needed: 'if one member suffers, all suffer together; if one member is honoured, all rejoice together' (I Corinthians 12: 12–26).

This approach to the 'other', which both St Paul's teaching and the concept of *ubuntu* express, has very far-reaching implications for relations within and between individuals, between individuals and their community, and between whole societies. Its valuing of each difference as equally essential to the health of the whole is crucially opposed to the understanding of difference as something fearful, to be rejected and even demonized. In the language of the blood-soul, explored in Chapter 4, *ubuntu* is the connecting energy that draws the disparate parts together to create a resonant whole, not only within individuals but between them.

The understanding of right relationship between people encoded in the concept of *ubuntu* seems universal, found across time and place – and Africa may be where it originated. Astrid Berg, a Jungian analyst in South Africa, cites the evidence that the first human beings came from this continent, and suggests that with them came a universal and basic human attitude that ensured the species' survival. This attitude, she says, is still alive in Africa today, a reminder to other cultures of what they have forgotten. As Nelson Mandela told the Oxford Centre for Islamic Studies, African religion has brought enrichment of humanity's spiritual heritage; *ubuntu* has added to the common search for a better world.[8]

Ubuntu is written into South Africa's constitution. It finds expression too in the legal system, under an earlier constitution which granted constitutional status to African customary law. As Alex Boraine, Vice-Chairman of the Truth and Reconciliation Commission, points out, *ubuntu* permeates the country's jurisprudence with three principles: communitarianism and emphasis on group solidarity rather than on individualism; conciliation and the restoration of peace rather than adversarial justice; and the promotion of the individual's duty to the larger group rather than individual rights. These principles also find expression in the proliferation of non-governmental organizations, of which South Africa has more than almost any country in the world. This state, for so long denied the right of democratic political expression, has in fact become a very strong civil society – one of the factors, thinks Boraine, that made possible the achievements of the Truth and Reconciliation Commission.[9]

So the spirit of *ubuntu* is perhaps what has made it possible for South Africa to survive.

A white woman visits a black township for the first time, just after the country's first democratic election. A small black boy peers at her over a wall and calls out something in Xhosa – to which a man opposite shouts back. The boy, she learns from her companion, had called out 'Look, a white woman!' The man had pulled him up: 'She is your mother.' Beyond all the differences, the man, who had known the inhumanity of apartheid, was affirming the spirit of *ubuntu* by teaching the child that any adult was to be honoured as his parent.[10]

The young black policeman, who had worked with the white security forces and participated in the murder of seven black men, meets with the mothers of some of them to ask forgiveness after his hearing at the Truth and Reconciliation Commission. He respectfully addresses them as 'my mothers'. In the midst of their grief, anger and questioning, they call him 'my son'.[11]

The mother of a young black man murdered by the security forces tells the commission of her feelings: 'This thing called reconciliation . . . if it means that this perpetrator, this man who has killed Christopher Piet, if it means he becomes human again, this man, so that, so that all of us get our humanity back . . . then I agree, then I support it all.'[12]

Nelson Mandela writes of his 27 years in prison under the apartheid regime:

> It was during those long and lonely years that my hunger for the freedom of my own people became a hunger for the freedom of all people, white and black. I knew as well as I knew anything that the oppressor must be liberated just as surely as the oppressed. I am not truly free if I am taking away someone else's freedom, just as surely as I am not free when my freedom is taken from me. The oppressed and the oppressor alike are robbed of their humanity.[13]

The Truth and Reconciliation Commission has drawn criticism since before it started, throughout its mandate and in the years since its report. From the very first lines of the first volume of its million-word main report, the commission made clear that its concern was with the suffering of all South Africans under apartheid, and with whoever was responsible: 'Our country is soaked in the blood of her children of all races and all political persuasions,' the Chairman's Foreword begins. Yet the poison of apartheid made that hard for all sides to believe. One major Afrikaans newspaper referred to it regularly as 'the commission for lies and revenge'. It never won more than grudging cooperation from Chief Buthelezi's Inkata Freedom Party, which it found to be second only to the apparatus of apartheid as a perpetrator of gross violations of human rights; it reckoned its failure to insist that Buthelezi appeared before it as one of its signal weaknesses.

The commission's findings were contentious even before they appeared. Unlike many others, this one was so scrupulous that it was obliged to give people the chance to make written reply to critical comments before publication. The former President, F. W. de Klerk, won a last-minute injunction to prevent inclusion of its findings on his responsibility for the actions of the apartheid state. The whole of the fifth volume of the report, already printed, had to be recalled and the offending page rewritten and handstitched back in; where the findings on de Klerk should have been, there is only a black square. The ANC missed the deadline for inclusion of comments on its own role in human rights violations, although it had already accepted the findings of its own earlier groundbreaking commissions into abuses by its members; it asked for a special meeting instead. The commission refused both this special treatment and consideration of the ANC's out-of-time written representation; this was the only time that Tutu used his chairman's casting vote. The ANC then also applied for a court injunction. It was only hours before the report was due to be presented to the president that the commission learned that the application had been dismissed with costs. So behind the handover ceremony's solemnity and celebration, tears and rejoicing, at which Desmond Tutu and Nelson Mandela so memorably danced together, was the sobering knowledge that the president's own party had wanted the occasion destroyed.

The commission was criticized for the way it went about its business, its findings – and the fact that it could not heal a nation's wounds. 'We've had the truth, there's even talk about reconciliation – but where's the justice?' became a familiar refrain. The commission itself was frank about its own failure to go as deeply into the complexities of apartheid as it would have wished. It forcefully regretted the failure of the white community, the beneficiaries as well as perpetrators of apartheid, to accept its repeated invitation to full participation. It regretted the way in which those granted amnesty benefited immediately while even urgent and modest reparations for their victims, who had lost any right to civil or criminal damages, got caught up in the bureaucratic delays of parliamentary procedure. This was the more poignant because often victims sought so little by way of reparation: funds for a child's education, the money for a tombstone, the return of a loved body, or even a bone of it, for burial. (One significant result of the amnesty hearings was the identification of hitherto secret mass graves; the bodies of 50 victims of the security forces were recovered and buried by their families.)

The delay in making reparation underlined the commission's insistence that the country could only be truly healed when economic and social justice was built into South African institutions. But its recommendations emphasized other values as well, inviting all South Africans to accept their own need for healing, and urging them to reach out to one another in a spirit of tolerance and understanding. The questions these recommendations raised were deep and lasting. In her own moving account, Antjie Krog, the poet and journalist who led the SABC reporting team throughout the commission's life, points out that the nature of reconciliation itself has had different interpretations: where for Desmond Tutu it is the beginning of a transformative process, for President Thabo Mbeki it could only become possible *after* social transformation had been achieved.[14] Ten years after the commission was set up, the commemoration of the country's official reconciliation day was sombre. Tutu regretted deeply the failure to bring to justice those who had refused to apply for amnesty and were known to have committed gross violations of human rights. At an official ceremony, President Mbeki questioned whether black and white South Africans, though under the same flag and anthem, were in fact still marching separately – 'even pretending at times that the other does not exist'.[15]

Yet the Truth and Reconciliation Commission made that pretence finally impossible. It changed the history of South Africa for all time: never again would people be able to say they 'didn't know' what happened under apartheid or to undo the truth of acknowledgement and justice of recognition which informed the victims' hearings.[16] For all the white community had never participated in the commission's work as it had hoped, the testimony of individual voices within it could not be ignored. One of the very early public hearings concerned a Christmas Day party at a golf club at which a grenade attack had left four guests dead. A white woman who had herself been grievously and lastingly injured in that attack told the hearing:

> I would like to meet the man who killed my friends and injured me. I would like to meet that man that threw that grenade in an attitude of forgiveness, and hope that he could forgive me too for whatever reason.[17]

As the commission's Vice-Chairman Alex Boraine wrote of this testimony, many people would strongly disagree with her sentiments. 'But in a few short, sensitive words she accepted the responsibility of the beneficiaries of apartheid for some of the horror and tragedy of the conflict which had raged in South Africa.'[18]

The commission ensured that the demands of reconciliation could not be ignored. For Boraine, its greatest contribution was its emphasis that these will never be easy, never cheap and will remain a constant challenge: 'Reconciliation is a process which engaged the energy of the commission but will always remain the responsibility of the entire nation.'[19] And for all the criticism of the amnesty provisions, these pointed the way to a different sort of justice. As Desmond Tutu wrote in his Foreword to the report:

> Certainly amnesty cannot be viewed as justice if we think of justice only as retributive and punitive in nature. We believe however that there is another kind of justice – a restorative justice which is concerned not so much with punishment as with correcting imbalances, restoring broken relationships – with healing, harmony and reconciliation. Such justice focuses on the experience of victims; hence the importance of reparation.[20]

The commission's attention to that experience found extraordinary expression in its published rollcall of those who had suffered gross violation of their human rights: their names alone took up 81 pages of the fifth volume of its report, and together with the briefest of summaries of their abuse the whole of the final volume. That insistence on respect for the individual, together with the recognition that no summary could express the fullness of their suffering, was also intrinsic to the hearings. The commission's emphasis on entering into and supporting the individual retelling of victims' experiences – often as real in their remembered details as if the horrifying events had happened only weeks before – led cynics to dub it 'the Kleenex commission'. It was said to be 'too religious' and criticized for its emphasis on reconciliation and *ubuntu*, instead of allowing room for justified anger. Yet time and again, victims especially vindicated its approach, with expressions of forgiveness as well as anguish, their witnessing audiences breaking spontaneously into hymns and prayers as well as tears. This was a process where the language of the blood-soul was given its place.

The commission's approach offered a *methodology* of reconciliation – both of individuals to themselves and of individuals to others. The unfailing respect shown to them and their experience could be healing in itself: as one woman said, it was the first time in her life that she had been invited to sit down by an 'official' body. Telling their story, having it intently heard in their own language and expression, could bring relief from years of suffering.

Lukas Baba Sikwepere became blind when police shot him in the face during a political conflict in 1985; two years later, police beat him with electric ropes, suffocated him, forced him to lie in an empty grave and further tortured him. 'I feel that what has been making me sick all the time,' he told the commission, 'is the fact that I couldn't tell my story. But now it feels like I got my sight back by coming here and telling you the story.'

Tim Legerwood, a former conscript in the South African Defence Force (open only to whites) went absent without leave in 1981 and when he tried to join the military wing of the ANC was caught and severely tortured by the security police. 'The commission has deeply affected my life,' he said, '. . . since I first . . . told my story to one of the investigators. It has begun a healing process in all sorts of relationships in my family and enabled me to begin on my own road to inner healing. . . . As if I've been freed from a prison in which I have been for eighteen years. It is also as if my family has been freed.'[21]

The commission's hearings decriminalized what were essentially moral and political acts; they exonerated the memory of those who had been falsely accused of collaboration with state forces. They gave victims the chance to express forgiveness and perpetrators to express remorse. Of course this did not always happen. One of the criticisms of the commission was that it encouraged people to reopen appalling wounds and then left them without any help to deal with their emotions, let alone come to the peace of forgiveness. This could affect perpetrators as well as victims. One man who had worked in a 'special unit' of the security forces wrote to Antjie Krog:

> They can give me Amnesty 1000 times. Even if God and everyone else forgives me 1000 times, I have to live with this hell. The problem is in my head, my conscience. There is only one way to be free of it. Blow my own brains out. Because that is where my hell is.[22]

This man believed that there could be no forgiveness for what he had done. But time and again, victims showed an extraordinary and humbling willingness to forgive, and perpetrators, albeit in far smaller numbers, to ask for it. Where people did reach out to each other, the effect could be profound.

In 1992, soldiers opened fire on an ANC protest march in Bisho, Eastern Cape. Twenty-eight unarmed protestors were killed, together with one soldier and a protestor who died of his injuries three years later. The commission's hearing on this massacre was at Bisho itself, in a packed hall. The already tense atmosphere tautened when the former head of the local military, Major General Marius Oelschig, expressed his regret for the loss of loved ones. He could not, he said, open his heart and put it out for public display; he was a soldier and had been taught to hide his tears and grieve alone. This soldier's creed incensed the audience, which heard it as hard and cynical. When Colonel Horst Schobesberger, who spoke for his black fellow officers, said that they had indeed ordered the soldiers to open fire, the audience could not have been more hostile. Then he said:

> I say we are sorry. I say the burden of the Bisho Massacre will be on our shoulders for the rest of our lives. We cannot wish it away. It happened. But please, I ask specifically the victims not to forget – I cannot ask this – but to forgive us, to get the soldiers back in the community, to accept them fully, to try to understand also the pressure they were under then. This is all I can do. I'm sorry, this I can say, I'm sorry.

His statement seemed to come at the right moment. It was a turning point. The audience burst into thunderous applause.[23]

The commission's work, which was in itself an example of the *process* of reconciliation, showed just how agonizing that process can be. The 17 commissioners found out very early that they were a microcosm of a society poisoned by apartheid. 'Our meetings for the first year or so,' says Desmond Tutu bluntly, 'were hell.' They were also exhausting, as the commission and those who served it travelled constantly in their determination to hold hearings throughout the country. People became cut off from their families both literally and emotionally, as the intensity of their experience became impossible to convey. They became ill. Tutu himself developed prostate cancer: while this probably would have happened anyway, he said, it also seemed to demonstrate that this was a costly procedure. During the 18 months of the hearings, the commissioners had to work constantly to restrain their own emotions of grief and anger, so as not to draw attention from their witnesses. The translators who had to recount in the first person tales of horrific torture, from both victims and perpetrators, could not keep themselves free of the horror and suffering. The people who made transcripts of the evidence didn't realize they were weeping until their tears fell on the paper. Antjie Krog broke down when she learned of her appointment as head of the SABC reporting team, and later had to endure a flood of hate mail. She describes how journalists, most of them also Afrikaners, began to get sicknesses, particularly in the lungs and airways, as if they couldn't breathe in the atmosphere of the hearings; they would try to distance themselves by watching proceedings on the monitors rather than going into the halls.

Through it all, extraordinary things were achieved. At the end of her own intense account of her years with the commission, Antjie Krog writes: 'The Commission has kept alive the idea of a common humanity. Painstakingly, it has chiselled a way beyond racism and made space for all our voices. For all its failures, it carries a flame of hope that makes me proud to be from here, of here.' She writes a poem 'for us all: all voices, all victims', that begins:

> because of you
> this country no longer lies
> between us but within. . . .[24]

The very first of the commission's public hearings set a tone that could hardly have been further from the deliberate objectivity of a court of law, a tone which illuminated its work right to the end. In the language of this book, the search for justice it exemplified was *themis* consciousness in action. This was a work, however painful, of the heart as well as the mind, the blood-soul as well as the spirit-soul. It brought together people whose very existence could represent to each other nothing but anger, fear and distress. It offered anything but rosy resolutions in its pursuit of truth, quoting God's injunction against those who have 'healed the wound of my people lightly, saying "Peace, peace" where there is no peace' (Jeremiah 8: 11). The recognition that remorse cannot be compelled and that false apology is worse than none at all was built into its process of amnesty. Forgiveness in this context was nothing sentimental, but a hard-won recognition that the desire to repay perpetrators in kind is only a further enslavement. As the sombre assessments of the commission's tenth anniversary emphasized, South Africans today are far from living in perfect harmony because of it. But the commission's achievement and challenge are not forgotten, and it has become an international model for peace-seekers. As Tutu says in his introduction to the sixth volume of its report:

> Quite improbably, we as South Africans have become a beacon of hope to others locked in deadly conflict that peace, that a just resolution is possible. If it could happen in South Africa, then it can certainly happen anywhere else. Such is the exquisite divine sense of humour.[25]

When he took that message to Northern Ireland, where generation after generation has played out ancient enmities in a deathly destruction of the very idea of shared community, it was heard, Tutu says, as if it had been uttered by an oracle. And perhaps it was from that deep place of wisdom which was once Themis's own that the message originated. Her oracle was less an encouraging foretelling of the future than a statement of what profoundly is. What the oracle tells here is that the psychological urge to come together towards wholeness and reconciliation, in both individuals and communities, is just as much a part of the human make-up as the urge towards destruction and revenge.

In March 2006, Archbishop Tutu chaired three sessions of reconciliation in

Northern Ireland for the British Broadcasting Corporation. Individuals from different sides of the conflict – Protestant, Catholic and British army – met together in front of the cameras. The programmes were contentious. Some people found them moving, even inspiring, others superficial and glib. They sparked a debate about the nature of forgiveness and whether some crimes are quite simply unpardonable. One columnist likened Tutu to a carrion crow, 'feeding on the corpses of human wickedness and sorrow'.[26]

But for the participants, the experience seemed different. Emotions were raw: sometimes the man whom relatives confronted had killed their husband or son. They heard each other's accounts of the fatal moments, with sometimes dramatic effect. One British ex-soldier came to accept that he had made a terrible mistake, and that the young man he had killed as a member of the IRA was in fact innocent, as his family had always maintained. Participants spoke of the weight of communal traditions and beliefs that had led people as young as 16, from both sides of the Northern Ireland divide, to join the political causes that turned them into murderers. They became more human to each other, and could accept Tutu's urging that they shake hands; two of them even said they would go for a drink together. In follow-up interviews on the BBC website, not one of those involved said they regretted it. Many victims experienced release from a past that had remained only too present for 20 years or more, even a vindication of their dead relative. Some, both victims and perpetrators, hoped that their example had done something for the cause of peace in Northern Ireland.[27]

'Confession, forgiveness and reconciliation in the lives of nations,' Desmond Tutu has said, 'are not just airy-fairy religious and spiritual things, nebulous and unrealistic. They are the stuff of practical politics.' This conviction is increasingly finding acceptance among academics and those concerned with the processes of peace. For one contributor to a volume of academic assessments of the South African experience, for instance, 'the belief that civil institutions are incapable of pursuing reconciliation reflects a failure of political imagination'.[28]

In 2005, Demos, a British 'think tank for everyday democracy', found that truth and reconciliation commissions performed an essential function in 'transitional justice'. But more than that, it argued for the vital importance of attention to the *human* aspects of security, which the TRC embodied. At the moment, governments pay these 'soft' aspects little heed: by 2005 for instance, the British government devoted less than half of one per cent of its military budget to conflict prevention and resolution – and it had a better record than all but the Scandinavian countries. But ultimately, the Demos authors argued, a decision will have to be made between the politics of threat and the politics of inclusion. While the first might seem effective in the short run, the long-term effect is likely to be an increase in the desire for retaliation and retribution. After a war, they say, reconstructing buildings is the easy bit, rebuilding societies is much more difficult:

What is most challenging and least attended to, are the deep wounds left in the hearts and minds of those who live on. If these wounds are left untreated, they fester into further horror. That's why skill and serious money must be invested in this healing, why human security is the issue of the time, and why war prevention is the coming science.[29]

In this work, the essential element is the human capacity to come together and contain warring opposites in a movement towards greater wholeness. This rests on and draws from the always present archetypal energy imaged so long ago by Themis. Is the wisdom of the goddess, which draws together and holds the energies of both heart and mind in her own 'right order', now becoming less hidden and more available to work for reconciliation and healing in the world?

Chapter 9

Invitation to the banquet

Themis does more than bring the Olympians together in council. She also convenes and presides over their feasts.[1] So this ancient energy, born of Earth, has a task of particular honour in the realms of the Heavens – and one which brings enjoyment and delight to all the other gods and goddesses. In psychological language, it seems that if we humans remain conscious of *themis* energy, then we too will be able to celebrate the feast which brings together different aspects of individuals, and individuals with each other, in all their diversity and similarity.

For human beings, sharing a meal with others is a fundamental coming together – and one that very few other species observe. The rituals of gathering round the family table, whether each day, each week or only once a year, still draw participants to affirm something important about their own identity through an evocation of a shared history. The unleavened bread and bitter herbs of Passover, the biryanis and sweetmeats of Eid ul-Fitr, the bread and wine of the Christian eucharist, the roast turkey and pumpkin pie of Thanksgiving – all play their ritual parts in bringing together communities, remembering peoples and their histories. Community feasts like the Mexican Day of the Dead are reminders too that the living are united not just with each other, but with their ancestral past.[2]

This coming together may be difficult. Individuals may come to celebratory tables with pleasurable anticipation or with resentment and dread. The memories they bring with them may be happy, poignant or hateful, and what is designed to unite may do the very opposite as old bitternesses are revived and old scores settled. The fact that family feasts are so often also the cue for family explosions is indication enough of their psychological power, as stories which have been repressed and denied may demand their place at the table. So coming together may not be easy, any more than it was for Diana to bring into consciousness the repressed experiences and hidden aspects of herself, or it is for participants in the different initiatives for restorative justice to sit together and be moved by each other's stories. The person we find ourselves next to at the feast may never become a friend of our heart: in the language of the blood-soul, there may never be much resonance between us. But if the different stories can be heard, rather than shut out like Strife from that Olympian wedding feast, then the result may be healing rather than another long-drawn, bloody, Trojan War.[3] At some deep level, people who eat together are united in a bond that goes beyond the personal: in many cultures, to fight against those with whom a meal has been shared is a breach not only of hospitality but of a human law which reflects something much more profound. People who break bread together are, quite literally, *companions*, brought together in a reciprocal bond of host and guest which also implies that they are both.

The rituals of preparing, serving and eating a meal may seem to deny this. The dietary laws and preferences for this dish or that can reinforce the sense of 'our people' as special and everyone else as odd, incomprehensible or simply barbaric. For the English, for instance, the French are 'frogs' and for the French the English are 'les rosbifs', and it will take more than the bureaucratic apparatus of the European Union to persuade them otherwise. But to understand the importance and meaning of the foods and feasts of others can also show something of the profound bond that lies between peoples, as Robin Soans' play *The Arab-Israeli Cookbook*, first produced in 2004, movingly shows. The play is based on interviews with Palestinians and Israelis – Jews, Muslims and Christians. They told of horror, anger and tragedy, but they also told of recipes and ingredients, of care and delight in preparing food for both simple meals and ritual celebrations – and so of the deeper human union that underlies the enmities. To prepare, serve and share a meal is also to participate in an act of transformation. This happens literally, as the raw food is transformed into the cooked, and the cooked food is digested and converted into energy. And it happens symbolically as well. Maybe the Western city dwellers' delight in the rich brew of 'ethnic' restaurants carries a more than gastronomic message in a world that is slowly learning to enjoy its own diversity.

The human capacity to come together in greater understanding of what constitutes a fuller humanity, and the potential for transformation which this brings, is what this book calls *themis* energy. It has explored the journey towards Themis's own 'right order', which brings together blood-soul and spirit-soul, among individuals and in societies. This 'right order' is anything but a static force, anything but rigid, judgemental or backwards looking. *Themis* energy is always dynamic, always moving both individuals and societies towards a greater integration. (Significantly, the approach of the many truth commissions which have helped move whole societies from tyranny towards a greater democracy is also known as '*transitional* justice'.) And it is through *themis* energy that humankind may also be led towards the tools it will need in a search for greater wholeness.

The most famous of Themis's children is Prometheus. Like her, he is a Titan, born before her union with Zeus, and so he carries the ancient blood-soul to a new generation. This maternal line is of prime importance to

Prometheus; he defines himself not by his father, but as the son of Themis or Earth, 'one person though of various names'. As 'the one who thinks ahead', he carries something of their ancient oracular power. But where Zeus will always bend to hear the wise counsel which Themis brings, he and Prometheus are always at odds, for the Titan's constant work is to advance humankind and diminish the power of the gods in their lives. In psychological terms, this is the energy which works to draw consciousness from its archetypal roots. The urge towards greater consciousness seems to be intrinsic to human beings: some even say that it was Prometheus who made humankind in the first place, fashioning them out of Mother Earth's own clay for Athene to ensoul with her breath.[4]

Zeus, like his father and grandfather before him, cannot bear challenge to his authority – and this one, which comes from humans rather than a new generation of gods, seems perhaps the most insulting of all. Although once he spares the human race from annihilation because of Prometheus's urgent plea, finally he cannot stand the Titan's threat. He has him chained agonizingly to a rock, where each night a vulture pecks at his liver, the seat of life. But already the Titan has done his work. He has tricked Zeus out of the best portion of the sacrifice, which for ever after is reserved for humans. He has sneaked up the back stairs to Olympus and stolen for them the gift of fire which Zeus so jealously guarded for himself. More than that, it was Prometheus, so he claims, who gave humans the mind and capacity to reason, without which they would not have understood fire's manifold potentials. He taught them the science of number too, and of writing and the healing arts, and of the rising and setting of stars; he taught them how to crawl out of their holes and build houses and ships.[5]

For some people, Prometheus has become the very image of the hubris of Western consciousness. He exemplifies its desire to take the power of creation and destruction for itself, its arrogant abuses of technical knowledge and its failure to understand and respect the underlying laws of the gods and of nature itself. It doesn't take much looking around the world to see those destructive forces at work. But the arrogance that steals fire from the gods also keeps humans warm and fed, and technologies that are used to exploit and destroy the natural balance can also be used to enhance life and health. Consciousness, in short, can be used either for good or for ill. Prometheus was proud to remember his maternal inheritance: so his inventiveness comes not only from the conscious mind, but is rooted in Themis's 'right order' and nature's laws. The arrogant ones may be not the Titan but the humans who have forgotten this and taken his gifts to abuse rather than maintain the natural balance.

The rediscovery and rehonouring of this 'right order' is a work of re-creation. This book began with the creation myths which brought Themis 'into the world', and so brought the psychological energy that she personifies into potential consciousness. But as we have also seen, these are not the only myths of beginnings which may need to be remembered. And now there is one more again, and this time it is Themis herself who joins with humankind in a work of re-creation.

There came a time when Zeus really did become enraged beyond bearing with an older human race. He found only impiety and wickedness among them and saw nothing for it but to wipe them out and start again. The other gods were doubtful: who would tend their altars, they wondered; would wild beasts take over the earth? But Zeus was persuasive. So the destruction began. Zeus shut up the winds that might otherwise have blown away the clouds, and the rains poured down. His brother Poseidon shook the earth and the seas, and oceans and rivers roared and rose. Before long, seals were swimming where goats had grazed and dolphins were bumping into the topmost branches of oak trees. Terrifyingly, it seemed no time at all before dwellings, then animals, and then people were swept away in the great flood. At last, only two humans were left alive – Deucalion, son of Prometheus, and his wife Pyrrha. As both were known for their piety and love for the gods, Zeus, his rage spent at last, relented. He released the winds to clear the storm clouds and once more it became possible to see the difference between heaven and earth. Poseidon blew his conch and the seas and rivers sank to their accustomed level. The tops of the trees, mud-covered and battered, at least became visible again.

By the greatest of good fortune, or perhaps simply in accordance with natural law, Deucalion and Pyrrha's little boat had been swept up to Mount Parnassus, above Delphi, and run aground on its rocky slopes. Immediately, they offered prayers to the deities of the mountain, and particularly to Themis in her powerhouse, her oracular shrine. Then, still entirely shaken by the realization that they were the only humans left alive, they resolved to ask the goddess how they might repair the destruction that had overcome their race. Timidly they approached her holy shrine, its gables still stinking with foul weeds and its altars unlit. The goddess took pity on them. She told them to leave the shrine, veil their heads, loosen their garments, and then throw behind them the bones of their mother.

Pyrrha was aghast, for to disturb her mother's bones was to risk the impiety of disturbing her ghost. But Deucalion knew that gentle Themis would never advise a guilty action. He worked out that the bones were in fact the stones embedded in Great Mother Earth herself. So they did as the oracle had bade them and amazingly, unbelievably, the stones they threw began to soften and grow and acquire shapes which before long were discernable as human. Then the stones which Deucalion had thrown became men, and his wife's became women. The sun began to warm the sodden earth, and out of the two great elements of heat and moisture came fertile seeds. Earth herself once more produced creatures both recognizable and new – including, some say, the great serpent Python whom Apollo later slew.[6]

So Themis showed humans how to re-create themselves, and Mother Earth herself once more became the creative force that she had been before the beginning of time. This story of an essential cooperation between the natural order of things and human beings in the work of creation is strikingly different both to others told in this book and to others again. This was not the only occasion, of course, on which a deity had despaired of his creation and resolved on an almighty purification. But in the story of the great flood sent by the Judeo-Christian God, both the destruction and the re-creation were in the hands of the deity himself. Where Themis actively engaged the last two humans in the re-creation of their kind through the gathering and scattering of the stones, God's careful instruction to the righteous Noah and his family to save one breeding pair of every creature demanded a more conserving, less initiatory obedience. As time goes on, human involvement in the work of creation will be seen as hubris. John the Baptist, for instance, will warn his hearers against any pride based on their descent from Abraham through an echo of Deucalion and Pyrrha's tale: he reminds them that God can even raise up children to the patriarch from the stones at their feet.[7]

Perhaps now, however, the psychological energies that are imaged in Themis can once more come to the aid of human consciousness. Perhaps in the continuing individual and collective work of bringing understanding and creativity from the archetypal, unconscious realm of the gods, there may also be a remembering and rehonouring of the goddess's 'right order', through attention to the language of the blood-soul as well as the spirit-soul, and to the values of the heart as well as the head. If Themis is disrespected or forgotten, she will turn not her gentle face, but her implacable one. When she is offended, then Nemesis appears, the 'Righteous Anger' of this daughter of deadly Night especially terrifying to those who violate nature's laws.[8] It can certainly seem that the retribution of Nemesis has been unleashed in the world today. Yet if Themis is honoured, as she was by Deucalion and Pyrrha, it seems that the work of re-creation can continue.

This book has explored examples of *themis* energy at work, in individuals, groups and even a whole society. It does not do to overestimate the influence of these examples or others like them. Diana, John and Jennifer discovered the psychologically and physically healing power of the energy which 'brings the gods together' and enables these energies to work with human consciousness towards a greater wholeness of personality. But countless other people are suffering the psychological and physical dis-ease that seems so ironic an accompaniment to Western affluence and comfort: while *individuals* may be healed, the *collective* within which they are contained seems to remain disordered. One path to the healing of that collective, through a justice which seeks to reunite rather than splitting apart, restore 'right order' rather than rest on retribution, is gathering strength in many countries of the world as reports of its effectiveness grow. Yet the human tendency to reject the 'evil other', rather than sit down with 'the enemy' and search for a shared humanity, can seem barely dented by such approaches, whether in playground or politics; the experimental community whose institutions are all based on restorative principles remains a hope rather than a reality.

The country that has come nearest to realizing that hope is probably South Africa. But despite its constitutional principles, the spirit of *ubuntu* which pervades them and the achievements of the Truth and Reconciliation Commission, the country's inhabitants still suffer huge inequalities, injustices and angers. It is hard to predict how these may be worked with in the future, or whether they may one day prove too great to be contained. In a 2007 speech, Mamphela Ramphele, a founder of the Black Power movement and now Vice-Chancellor of Cape Town University, has spoken of the way in which her country's history has left many citizens, both white and black, convinced that there is an unbridgeable gulf between them and 'the other', and correspondingly intolerant to the diversity which the country must encompass. The stereotyping that has come with racist and sexist propaganda about superiority and inferiority have left their scars: black men who react very strongly against any suggestion that they might be inadequate in their public roles can still express deeply sexist views about women as leaders; white women who are very sensitive to the impact of sexism in their own lives find nothing wrong with their own racist views about black people. At the same time, it seems very hard for black people to voice any criticism of the political establishment without being labelled as traitors to their own – or even collusive with a white belief about black inferiority.[9]

The sufferings of the troubled world may seem to confirm that, in the imagery of kundalini yoga, warring nations and their individual citizens are often painfully and destructively stuck in the *manipura* chakra: the fiery whirlpool of emotional reaction can seem all-consuming, stifling the ability to reflect. Yet while it does not do to overestimate the 'bringing together' which *themis* energy has achieved, it does not do to underestimate it either. In the myriad acts of *themis* consciousness, and through the inseparable interplay of personal and collective psyche, individuals and the communities to which they belong are becoming more whole.

This movement towards healing can be seen, to take one instance, in the stories collected by the Forgiveness Project. These are the basis for its work in prisons, schools and faith communities at the grassroots of conflict resolution, reconciliation and victim support. The stories tell of individuals' struggles to live and work with the people and events that have destroyed lives most precious to them. Sometimes the tragedy is intensely personal, as it was for the parents of the eight-year-old girl, sent from southern Africa to 'a better life' in Britain, only to be horrendously tortured until her death by the aunt to whom she was entrusted. Sometimes the personal tragedies touch more nearly on the collective political world – like those of the young man who contracted HIV while in a Romanian orphanage, and the entire family reduced to invalidism in the wake of the nuclear disaster in their home town of Chernobyl. Sometimes again the personal tragedies are the direct result of political action – like those of both Protestants and Catholics in Northern Ireland, of the young woman who lost both legs in a London suicide bomb attack in 2005 that killed and injured many, and of the mother of a young man killed in the 2001 attack on the World Trade Center in New York.

Each of these individuals tells of their own ways of trying to understand and work with their tragedy. The parents of that little girl are raising money for a local school to give children the chances they hoped they had secured for their own daughter. The young man from the Romanian orphanage is learning slowly to understand the economic and social pressures that led his mother to abandon him, and to build some relationship with her. The father of the family from Chernobyl tells how they have never received one word of apology or remorse for the event that shattered their lives: 'So I do not forgive those who were responsible. Would you?' The young woman who lost her legs in the London bombings has come to her own understanding: 'The cycle has to stop – I cannot hate the person who has done this to me; the cycle must end with me. I don't see it as my place to forgive the act, yet I am compelled to understand – to offer an open heart to try to hear and ask Why?' The Jewish mother of the young man who died in the World Trade Center has forged a friendship with the devastated Muslim mother of one of those responsible for the destruction, begun when she offered support during the time of his trial. 'I have come to see forgiveness,' she says 'as more than a word. It's a context, a process. I do not forgive the act but trying to understand why someone has acted in the way he has is part of the process of forgiving. Forgiveness is being able to accept another person for being human and fallible.'[10]

The desire to come together, to understand each other and to reach a shared humanity, seems as much part of the human psychological make-up as the tendency to split apart from 'the stranger' in fear and mistrust, and project on to that 'evil other' all that is intolerable in oneself. And the desire to come together may be the more fundamental. In Corinth, in the sacred grove of Aesculpius the healer, Themis was worshipped together with Aphrodite.[11] The coming together of these two deities, both far more ancient than the Olympians, 'born' from Earth and Heaven, suggests something about the process of healing and making more whole. This seems to have to do with understanding both the underlying natural law of human beings and the powerful psychological energy of attraction and love between them. It tells not just of the 'right order' of nature but of human delight in that order, and celebration of the huge variety of the sensual world of which all are part.

This sense of celebration is encoded in the very interactions between body and mind: in the language of the blood-soul, states of *coherence* and *resonance* 'feel' good. Quite simply, humans like to feel 'in the flow' with themselves and others. Modern, individualistic Western psychology has been pervaded by the assumption that infants relate at first only to one other person, and this has underwritten the notion that the essential human relationship is lastingly between self and 'the other'. But recent observation has shown that in fact infants are able from the start to relate to more than one other person. This 'new' discovery evokes an old truth. As the philosophy of *ubuntu* expresses it, 'a person is a person because of other people'; somewhere we 'know' that our personhood is inextricable from that of others.[12]

The desire to come together finds expression not just in countless individual lives but in philosophies that link them over time and place. As we have seen, it has been suggested that *ubuntu* may even have been encoded into the psychology of our human race since its African beginnings. It may still be the sturdiest foundation for living together in an immensely complicated and divided world. As Kwame Anthony Appiah, professor of philosophy at Princeton University, points out, global communications now enable more and more of us to learn about each other, and the actions of our governments can now affect the lives of millions for good or ill. This has huge moral implications:

> Each person you know about and can affect is someone to whom you have responsibilities: to say this is just to affirm the very idea of morality. The challenge, then, is to take minds and hearts formed over the long millennia of living in local troops and equip them with ideas and institutions that will allow us to live together as the global tribe we have become.[13]

In his own eloquent search for 'ethics in a world of strangers', Appiah turns to 'cosmopolitanism'. To the Cynics in the fourth century BCE, this philosophy had nothing to do with the superiority of the jet-set life or disparaging the untravelled. Its assertion that we are all citizens not of a particular state or nation, but of the cosmos itself, was taken up by the Stoics; from there it informed Christianity, and over the centuries the many movements towards a recognition of universal human rights. In his own expression of the obligations that come with this universal citizenship, the eighteenth-century philosopher Voltaire posed a question that is being echoed by Fair Trade campaigners to this day:

> Fed by the products of their soil, dressed in their fabrics, amused by the games they invented, instructed even by their ancient fables, why would we neglect to understand the mind of these nations, among whom our European traders have travelled ever since they could find a way to get to them?[14]

For Appiah, the first step towards a new cosmopolitanism is *conversation*. This, as he emphasizes, brings no promise of final agreement – whether between friends or among strangers. But it does begin that process of *getting used* to each other and to other ways of being and doing, which in turn can lead to a change in our own habits of action and mind. Importantly, this does not mean searching for a uniformity of either. One of cosmopolitanism's basic commitments is to a recognition that there are many values worth living by and that each must be respected. In a slogan, it is about 'universality plus difference'. Turning the slogan into reality, discerning through our conversations which values *are* worth living by and according them respect, seems to be among the most urgent of contemporary tasks, for both individuals and societies. As Mamphela Ramphele says of the hugely diverse and often fragmented society that is South Africa: 'the challenges of identity as a nation are not necessarily related to the multiplicity of fragments, but to the willingness to accept that multiplicity of identities can co-exist within a united nation'.[15]

The willingness and capacity to work with this apparent paradox, to bring together and hold multiplicity in unity seems to be exactly the work of *themis* energy, among both individuals and the societies of which they are a part. As we have seen, the goddess has many of the attributes that Jung attributed to the Self, the archetype of orientation and meaning which both encompasses the totality of psyche and leads to its centre. This central archetype, Jung wrote in 1959, 'plays the chief role in uniting apparently irreconcilable opposites and is therefore the best suited to compensate the split-mindedness of our age'.[16] Fifty years on, the age seems no less 'split-minded' and the need for a unifying force just as urgent. In the stories of Themis we can perhaps now understand more of the way it operates.

When Themis calls the gods to council, she does not then impose agreement among them. As Diana knew, her journey was not towards the abolition of difference between her psychological energies, but living with their diversity in greater harmony. The participants in different schemes for restorative justice do not end up concluding that they are 'just like' each other – though they may discover that they are more alike than they first thought – but they do very often end up understanding more about each other's lives and struggles. This may or may not lead to 'forgiveness' and reconciliation – though as Appiah points out, 'we often *do* forgive, once we understand'.[17] But at the very least, Themis's 'calling together' of the gods to council makes it possible to begin the conversations which are the prelude to the re-creation of individual and collective worlds.

These potentially transformative conversations within individuals and between them may also extend to the communities of which they are a part. To take one example, Search for Common Ground (SFCG) has been working for over 20 years to transform adversarial approaches to conflict into collaborative problem solving. Its starting point – 'understand the differences, act on the commonalities' – is exactly the honouring of both diversity and similarity about which Appiah is talking and which *themis* energy seems to encompass and encourage. In 2007, some 350 people, mostly drawn from local populations, were working in 17 different countries to bring together communities which had been bitterly torn apart. SFCG's 'toolbox' runs from shuttle diplomacy between Israel and Palestine to educational soap opera in

Sierra Leone, from education in mediation skills in the Ukraine to bilingual kindergarten in Macedonia. Anecdotal evidence and self-scrutiny indicate that the approach seems to work, by above all reducing fear, misapprehension and suspicion between different groups as a foundation for advancing peace processes, reducing violence, and equipping communities with the capacity to resolve conflict.[18]

There can be no knowing where the conversations within and between individuals and communities will take them, or what the cumulative effect of such meetings might be. But the early meanings of the word perhaps offer a clue that the journey may lead well beyond exchanges of views, opinions and beliefs. 'Conversation' means 'frequent abode' and comes to signify living, having one's abode – including spiritual abode – 'among persons'. It has to do with citizenship, an individual's engagement with people and things. This engagement and abode may go well beyond the boundaries of city or nation: 'our conversation is in heaven' as one seventeenth-century theologian said. In the Western understanding of kundalini yoga, this deep level of 'conversation' may lie in the realm of *vishuddha* chakra, where the individualistic or nationalistic view is transcended and there is a perception of the interconnectedness of inner and outer, individual and collective. Appiah's own experience of the 'adventure and ideal' of cosmopolitanism evokes something of what 'conversations' at these levels may bring. He himself is a true cosmopolitan: the son of a Ghanaian father and English mother, he was educated in both their countries and is also immersed in the rich cultural diversity of his home town. He brings all this together to show how such a feast of different beliefs, values and experiences can enrich and nourish – and offers fond memories of literal feasting as well, in the celebrations of Eid al-Fitr at the house of his Christian Auntie Grace and devoutly Muslim Uncle Aviv.

They say that the banquet Themis prepared for the wedding of Thetis and Peleus, the one where Strife wound up the sufferings of the Trojan war, was also the last time that the gods and humans sat down to share a meal. But although there can be no returning to that Golden Age when humans lived like gods, some of the recipes for coming together towards the nourishment of 'right order' now seem available to human consciousness. These are what this book has been about, and one of them has already been explored in this chapter: an understanding that similarity and diversity are equally the building blocks of relationship. Another has also run insistently through these pages: the need to bring together once more the blood-soul and the spirit-soul, which have become so split apart in the developing story of Western consciousness, and to be informed by both. As Appiah says, the challenge of learning to live together as a global tribe is one for mind and heart.

When Themis arrived on Olympus, she became the mediator between the old Titanic order and the new. The image of her sitting beside Zeus, as they lean together in wise counsel, is of the union of the two souls, a cooperation between body and mind. This relationship is one which Themis seems to want to foster. In later tales, she attends the birth of Apollo and with her own hands feeds him his first sips of nectar and ambrosia; she watches with amazement and pleasure as he immediately bursts out of his swaddling bands and strides out over the wide paths of the earth.[19] This story tells that the goddess is involved at the very birth and development of intellectual capacity, and takes delight in its growth. So *themis* energy continues to bring together heart-soul and spirit-soul, emotion and rationality, and this healing bridge can lead to exciting new discoveries about human beings and how they may relate to each other. As we have seen, it is precisely the tools and technologies developed by the highest arts of Apollonian intellect that are helping to deepen understanding of the language of the blood-soul.

As we have seen too, this language from the body and the emotions has traditionally been associated with 'the feminine', just as the spirit-soul has been associated with 'the masculine'. There can be no doubting the far-reaching effect of 2000 years and more of certain belief that the body is inferior to the spirit – the lives of countless individual men and women, the over-rationality of Western consciousness, and the exploitation of Mother Earth herself have all been shaped by it. But now the old certainties have been disrupted. The plight of the earth has given an urgent impetus to today's often angry, often perplexing, sometimes fearful attempts to reach a new understanding of what 'masculine' and 'feminine' might mean. Whether in private lives or public institutions, individual relationships, social structures or world economics, there seems to be a common theme: a growing awareness that for the sake of this planet and its peoples there needs to be a new balance between the 'feminine' values of the heart and the 'masculine' ones of the head, the feelings and the intellect. More than 25 years ago, the philosopher Richard Tarnas wrote *The Passion of the Western Mind*. It was a best-seller then and its central premise seems prescient now. For him, the 'new' awareness may in fact have been embedded all along: the Western mind's deepest passion is and always has been, he says, 'to reunite with the ground of its own being'. 'The driving impulse of the West's masculine consciousness has been its dialectical quest not only to realise itself, to forge its own autonomy, but also, finally, to come to terms with the great feminine principle in life, and thus to rediscover its connection to the whole.'[20]

This 'profound and many-levelled marriage of the masculine and feminine, a triumphant and healing reunion' foreseen by Tarnas has its own deep history, and it is one that is told across time and space. The ancient Eastern discipline of kundalini yoga, as we have seen, can be understood as a process of making conscious the divine union of Shiva and Shakti, the masculine and feminine principles. Prefigured in the 'root support' of the *muladhara* chakra in the lingam and kundalini serpent, this union becomes conscious in the *ajna* chakra as the adept becomes conscious of consciousness itself. For the Western alchemists at work over centuries in their laboratories, it was just this *heiros gamos*, the sacred marriage of masculine and feminine, spirit and matter, that would bring to birth the 'uncommon gold' of a new understanding of the nature of creation.

The alchemists drew on the ancient and universal symbolism of the sacred marriage of Sun and Moon. Today, thanks to the achievements of Apollonian reason, this can be seen from a radically and literally new perspective. As Jungian analyst Jules Cashford emphasizes in her deep study of the Moon, our age has a unique vision: for the first time we have seen Earth from the outside and as a whole, and it is the Moon – for millennia a symbol of transformation – which has made that possible:

> For the first time we were able to contemplate our own home, not forever looking out at somewhere else and far away. At the deepest level this is an image of consciousness reflecting on itself . . . This image allows Earth to become again both numinous and personal, with the radical difference that this Earth is no longer the local piece of territorial earth as in former days, but the unified Earth in which everyone shares and for which everyone is responsible.[21]

There is no way of knowing where these new visions and awarenesses may lead. But in a potentially far-reaching example of the 'bringing together' that this book sees as *themis* energy at work, Jungian analyst Jerome Bernstein writes of a new level of consciousness which seems to go beyond the individual to express a collective evolutionary shift. Drawing on the experience of people with whom he has worked, he detects the emergence of a new level of 'borderland' consciousness which is making connection with the 'transrational reality' of nature itself. These are people who do not just suffer for the ills done to the natural world; they actually live the suffering in their own bodies and psyches, in an experience not of regressive fantasy, neurotic overidentification or any other psychopathology, but of profound reconnection to the natural ground from which the Western mind has been so long estranged. In his own search for understanding of such phenomena as 'environmental illness complex' – that often baffling and profoundly debilitating variety of conditions which now affects an estimated 6 per cent of the US population – Bernstein turns to the still-living Navajo understanding that much illness results from a wound to or from nature itself. This understanding is now, he argues, returning to the Western psyche as the Western ego evolves. While those who live on the 'borderland' are the pioneers of this emerging consciousness, we are all involved in its unfolding – and it may be on this that the future of the species depends.[22]

This book offers its own images of the reunion of nature and culture – a reunion which is encoded in the physiology of each individual body as well as experienced in the understandings of the conscious mind. The marriage of Themis and Zeus brings not just the wise counsel that results from a resonance between blood-soul and spirit-soul, but the promise of the 'right order' which will flow from this. From this union of the masculine and feminine, as we have seen, come those three beautiful daughters – Eunomia, Eirene and Dike, Good Order, Peace and Justice. And their nature seems to speak of not just the goal they represent but also the process of reaching it. Together, these three are the Horai, and they have a very particular relationship with time. They are the Seasons, the Hours, and, even more precisely, the 'right moment'. So associated with their mother's deep order, it seems, is an attention to when the time is right. The importance of this has been intuited across time and place: as the author of Ecclesiastes has it, for instance, 'For everything there is a season, and a time for every matter under heaven' (Ecclesiastes 3:1).

The 'right moment' is transformative, as Diana and Jennifer experienced when dreams came to forge a vital new conscious connection to the blood-soul. John experienced a moment of heart-to-heart coherence with Pamela which enabled him to dissolve his destructive self-protective paranoia. At that community meeting, the young girl whose photo album had been destroyed in the school fire seemed to arrive at just the right moment to turn the closed cynicism of the perpetrators into constructive remorse. And when that South African commanding officer made his apology to the people of Bisho, it seemed to come at the right moment to transform their fury and distress into a rush of acceptance. In the language of the blood-soul, we can imagine that in all these instances moments of coherence between heart and mind created states of inner and outer resonance. We can also imagine what might have happened if there had not been that profound 'coming together'. The dreams of Diana and Jennifer would likely not have been brought to consciousness to do their transformative work; John might well have experienced Pamela's perception of his inner state as yet another dangerous attack on his self-defence system; the girl who showed her photo album could have been painfully rewounded by the cynicism of the perpetrators; the rage and anguish of the people of Bisho might have been dangerously fuelled by yet more seemingly empty words.

So it seems that the way towards the Horai lies through learning to become more aware of the 'right moment' – and this is something which they themselves will foster, as they roll back the clouds that obscure the realm of the gods from human sight. The huge abstractions of Good Order, Peace and Justice may appear remote from the small lives of individuals. But as this book has tried to show, attention to the language of the blood-soul and a growing understanding of the 'marriage' between the laws of the body and those of the mind may slowly bring us nearer to understanding what they might mean. So may spending time with the imagery that seems to reflect something of the 'right order' that underlies them. Through the evocation of Themis's attributes and deeds, and of the serpent of life as it winds through West and East, we have tried to kindle a reimagination of different ways of being. Importantly, the very fact that these old stories exist must mean that they are already somewhere encoded in the potential of the human psyche. The instances we give of the sudden movement of potential into embodied experience, in the transformative 'right moment' within and between individuals, seem to come as unbidden moments of grace. But if humans can attend to these moments and try to understand them, as Deucalion and Pyrrha attended to the altar of Themis, then perhaps more of the re-creative energy personified by the goddess may consciously unfold. Who knows what the cumulative collective impact of this work of individual consciousness might be? The right person sitting in their house and thinking the right thought may indeed be heard 100 miles away.[23]

Themis's 'right order', which holds in balance nature and culture, body and mind, the values of the heart and those of the head, is continuously evolving. It moves towards one new stage of integration and balance between these forces, and then, as inner and outer worlds change again, towards another which in turn is the 'right order' for its time and place. No one can know where the path will end, or even what the journey might finally mean for the way of the world and the individuals who inhabit it. But in that journey, *themis* energy can be a guide. And we might remember too that if ever we encounter Good Order, Peace and Justice along the way, we can surely trust them: one thing that everyone knows about these daughters of Themis is that they always tell the truth.

Notes

Prologue

1 Kerenyi, *The Gods of the Greeks*, p.102; Hesiod, ed. West, *Theogony*, p.408.
2 Campbell, *The Hero with a Thousand Faces*, p.13.
3 Jung, 13: 54.
4 Jung, 5: 337, 8: 339.
5 Hillman, 'Once more into the fray', p.12; Vannoy Adams, *The Mythological Unconscious*.
6 Jones, 'Jung's view of myth and post-modern psychology'.
7 Giegerich, 'The end of meaning and the birth of man'.
8 Jung, 5: xxiv–xxv; see Shearer 'On the making of myths', for a further development of this theme.
9 Jung, 9i: 271; Otto, quoted in Hillman, *The Myth of Analysis*, pp.207–208; Armstrong, *A History of God*, p.244.
10 One question about this much debated concept is whether it should be spelt with an upper or lower case 's'. We use the upper case, to distinguish it more clearly from a conscious, personal sense of self. Jung's translators, however, favour the lower case, and we follow that when quoting directly from his work, or from that of others who follow the same convention.
11 Jung, *Letters* 2, p.84.
12 Jung, 13: 242, 12: 157; Singer and Kimbles, *The Cultural Complex*.
13 Jung, *Visions Seminars*, p.506; Jung, 10: 45, 10: 778–780.
14 Hesiod, *Theogony*, trs. Wender, p.30; Graves, *Greek Myths*, Vol. 1, pp.125–6; Kerenyi, *Gods of the Greeks*, pp.105–8.

1 Birth of a goddess

1 Von Franz, *Creation Myths*, p.1.
2 Hesiod, ed. West, *Theogony*, p.46.
3 This story is taken from Hesiod, *Theogony*, trs. Wender.
4 See Baring and Cashford, *Myth of the Goddess*.
5 Jung, 10: 275.
6 Hesiod, trs. Wender; Graves, *The Greek Myths*, Vol. 1, pp.39–41.
7 Tarnas, *Passion of the Western Mind*, pp.441–442.
8 For the significance of the death of Tiamat and the story of the long, slow development of the patriarchal religions out of the rule of the ancient goddess, see Baring and Cashford.
9 Augustine, *City of God*, Vol. 1, p.124; Aquinas, quoted in Baring and Cashford, p.521 and Phillips, *Eve*, p.35; Hillman, *Myth of Analysis*, p.218.

10 Kerenyi, *Gods of the Greeks*, p.255.
11 Graves, *The Greek Myths*, Vol. 1, p.27; Brumble, *Classical Myths and Legends*, p.138.
12 Hesiod, *Theogony*, pp.46–47.
13 Kerenyi, p.20, pp.254–255.
14 *Ibid.* p.20; Lopez-Pedraza, *Dionysus in Exile*, p.9.
15 Freud, *New Introductory Lectures*, p.106.
16 Jung, 8: 281, 8: 406.
17 Jung, 10: 53, 10: 661.

2 The return from Tartarus

1 Hesiod, trs. Wender, *Work and Days*; Otto, *The Homeric Gods*, p.133.
2 Dodds, *The Greeks and the Irrational*, p.16.
3 Edinger, *The Psyche in Antiquity*, Book Two, p.72.
4 Jung, 6: 368.
5 Klossow de Rola, *Alchemy*, p.8; Read, *Prelude to Chemistry*, p.73.
6 Thomas, *Religion and the Decline of Magic*; Warner, *From the Beast to the Blonde*, pp.14–16.
7 Thomas, *Religion*, p.727; *MND*, IV, I, V.i.
8 Jung, 15: 4.
9 Edinger, *The Eternal Drama*, p.134.
10 Gimbutas, *Goddesses and Gods*; Yates, *Astraea*, p.32, p.34.
11 Jung, *Nietzche's Zarathustra*, 1, p.750, p.748.
12 Jung, 6: 801, 9i: 221, 7: 318, 245f, 247, 305, 307.
13 Teicher *et al.*, 'Wounds that time won't heal', *Cerebrum* 2(4), pp.50–67.
14 *Ibid.* p.65; Lieberman *et al.*, 'Putting feelings into words', *Psychological Science* 18(5), pp.421–428.
15 Kalsched, *The Inner World of Trauma*, pp.3–4.

3 Themis calls the gods together

1 Pindar, 2, *Fragment 30*, pp.232–233; Hesiod, *Theogony*, trs. Wender, p.30, p.52.
2 Aeschylus, *Prometheus Bound*, p.27; Pausanias, 1, p.61.
3 Cashford, *Homeric Hymns*, XXIII; Homer, *Iliad*, p.366; Kerenyi, *Gods*, p.102.
4 Kerenyi, *ibid.*; Hesiod, *Theogony*, p.52; Homer, *Iliad*, p.112.
5 Jung, 10: 275.
6 Jung, 13: 335.
7 Jung, *Kundalini Yoga*, p.49; Mindell, *Dreambody*, pp.42–43.
8 Baring and Cashford, *Myth*, p.111; Graves, *Myths*, 1, pp.75–76; Shearer, *Athene*, pp.67–68 for further tales about what happened to the vials of blood.
9 Baring and Cashford, *Myth*; Cooper, *Encyclopaedia*; De Vries, *Dictionary*.
10 See Chapter 2.
11 Jung, 9i: 629, 645; Jung, *Memories*, pp.221–224.
12 Jung, 9i: 634.
13 *The Collected Works* use the lower case 's'. We use the upper case to distinguish Jung's concept more clearly from others, except when we are quoting.
14 Jung, *Memories*, pp.224–225; Jung, 16: 474; Serrrano, *C.G. Jung and Herman Hesse*, quoted in Salman, 'Dissociation and the self'; Jung, 8: 817.
15 Jung, *Letters* 2, p.84.
16 Jung, 13: 242, 12: 157.

17 Cooper, *Encyclopaedia*; De Vries, *Dictionary*; The Archive for Research in Arche-typal Symbolism (*www.ARAS.org*); Jung, 8: 871, 9i: 425–426, 10: 692.

18 Adapted by the authors from the story in Graves, *Greek Myths* 1, p.27.

4 The language of the blood-soul

1 Much of the material on the heart has been taken from the research of the Institute of HeartMath. The articles referenced and others may be found at *www.HeartMath.org*.

2 McCraty and Childre, *The Appreciative Heart*, p.1.

3 McCraty, *The Energetic Heart*, p.3.

4 *Ibid.*, p.4; Jung 8: 200, 203; McCraty, *Heart Rhythm Coherence Feedback*, p.5.

5 *The Energetic Heart*, p.1, p.4; Jung, *Nietzsche's Zarathustra*, 1, p.750, p.748.

6 *The Appreciative Heart*, p.8; Davidson, 'Anterior electrophysiological asym-metries', pp. 607–614; Lane, 'Neuroantomical correlates of pleasant and unpleasant emotion', pp. 1437–1444.

7 *The Appreciative Heart*, p.16; *The Energetic Heart*, p.5, p.15.

8 *Ibid.*, p.1.

9 *Ibid.*, p.13.

10 *Ibid.*, p.8; Levenson and Gotman, 'Physiological and affective predictors'.

11 Jung, 14: 604n.

12 *The Energetic Heart*, pp.8–9.

13 Lewis, Amini and Lannon, *A General Theory of Love*, p.195.

14 McKenna, 'Sleep and arousal patterns', *American Journal of Physical Anthropol-ogy*, 83(3), pp.331–347.

15 Billy Collins, 'Another Reason Why I Don't Keep a Gun in the House', in *The Apple That Astonished Paris*.

16 Sanella, *The Kundalini Experience*, pp.7–8; Shamdasani, *The Psychology of Kundalini Yoga*, p.xxv; Rawson, *Tantra*.

17 Jung, in Shamdasani, p.xxi. Gopi Krishna, *Kundalini*, with a commentary by James Hillman, offers a rich comparison of the two disciplines, based on the profound experiences of the author.

18 Jung, in Shamdasani, p.106, p.21.

19 Sanella, pp.27–29; Jung, *Lectures I–IV*, and p.21 in Shamdasani; Jung, 16: 560–561.

20 Jung, in Shamdasani, p.xxix, p.70.

21 Sanella, pp.7–8; Jung, in Shamdasani, p.xlv.

5 The voice of the goddess

1 Herodotus, *Histories*, p.58.

2 Roux, *Greece*, p.134; Sheldon, *Greece*, p.84; Pendazos and Sarla, *Delphi*, p.46.

3 Aeschylus, *Prometheus Bound*, p.27; Hesiod, *Theogony*, trs.Wender, p.27; Fonten-rose, *The Delphic Oracle*, p.203; Sheldon, p.83; Geldard, *Traveller's Key*, p.262.

4 Neumann, *Great Mother*, p.138.

5 Kerenyi, *Gods*, p.136; Ovid, *Metamorphoses*, ed. More, p.37.

6 Freud, 'Dreams and telepathy', p.421; Heraclitus quoted in Wood, *The Road to Delphi*, p.43.

7 Jung, 8: 817, *Memories*, p.185, italic added; Plato, *The Last Days of Socrates*, pp.50–52.

8 Jung, 12: 44, 14: 41; 132n.

9 From Yeats' 'The Second Coming', in *Collected Poems*, p.184.

10 Heelas and Woodward, *The Spiritual Revolution*.
11 *www.drepung.org*.
12 Aeschylus, *Eumenides*, pp.9–10.
13 Cashford, *Homeric Hymns* III, p.46.
14 *Ibid.*, p.47.
15 Baring and Cashford, *Myth*, p.274.
16 *Ibid.*, p.522; Fontenrose, *Python*, pp.95–100; Begg, *Cult*, pp.40–41.
17 Euripides, *Iphigeneia in Tauris*, pp.171–172; Pendazos and Sarla, p.28.
18 Pausanias, *Guide* 1, p.416, p.468; Fontenrose, *Python*, p.374.
19 Partin, 'Ka'bah' in Eliade, *Encyclopaedia; Encyclopaedia Judaica*, p.16.
20 *http:// newsvote.bbc.co.uk*, 21.09.05.
21 Von Franz, *Alchemy*; Stalley, *Early Medieval Architecture*, pp.62–63.
22 Pendazos and Sarla, pp.101–102; Pausanias 1, p.468.
23 Aeschylus, *Eumenides*, p.9.
24 Roux, p.134; Wilhelm, *I Ching*, pp.193–197; Eberhard, *Dictionary*, p.299, p.241.
25 Parke, *History*, pp.386–387; Fontenrose, *Delphic Oracle*, pp.25–26; Miller, *Greek Horizons*, p.130.
26 Parke, p.393.
27 Jung, 11: 392, 14: 778; Huskinson, 'The self as violent other'.
28 Sheldon, pp.83ff; Parke, p.294; Fontenrose, *Python*, p.374. AS had the tripod-leg pointed out to her by a guide in 2003, with every appearance of seriousness.
29 Parke, p.295.
30 Warner, *Beast*, p.3, pp.67–79.
31 Rossiter, *Greece*, p.401; Pausanias 2, p.205; *www.olympic.org*.

6 Yearning for justice

1 Homer, *Odyssey*, p.39; Harrison, *Themis*, p.485; Pindar 1, *Olympian Ode 8*, p.139.
2 *Harper's Magazine*, February 2006 cover.
3 Hesiod, *Work and Days*, trs. Wender, pp.62–65; Ovid, *Metamorphoses*, trs. Innes, p.33; Kerenyi, *Gods*, pp.102–103.
4 Kramer, *Sumarian Mythology*, frontispiece; O'Neill, *Towards Justice*, p.9.
5 Zimmer, *Myths and Symbols*, p.15.
6 Jung, 6: 355, 6: 192.
7 Milton, 'On the Morning of Christ's Nativity', XV.
8 Heraclitus, quoted by Lloyd Jones, *The Justice of Zeus*, p.166; Conti, quoted by Brumble, *Classical Myths*, pp.38–39.
9 Jung, 9ii: 48, 10: 856, 11: 394.
10 Stein, *Solar Conscience*, p.55, p.57; Hesiod, *Work and Days*, trs. Wender, p.67.
11 Stein, *supra*.
12 Yates, *Astraea*, p.33.
13 Virgil, *Eclogues*, p.57.
14 Yates, pp.32–35.
15 Ficino, *Letters*, pp.146–147.
16 Yates, pp.59–69.
17 De Pizan, p.14; Yates, p.65.
18 Lurker, *Gods and Symbols*, p.78; Cashford, *Moon*, pp.250–251.
19 Ripa, *Iconologia*, p.120.
20 Ripa, *ibid.*; de Pizan, p.14.
21 Unless otherwise indicated, this and following information on images of justice is taken from Curtis and Resnik, 'Images of justice', and Johnson, 'Feminine origins of justice and law'.

22 Kramer and Sprenger, *The Malleus Maleficarum*, pp.6–7.
23 Jung, 9ii: 107–108.
24 Warner, *Monuments*, p.157; *Handbook of the Bombay Presidency*.
25 Warner, pp.64–65.
26 Freud, 'Psychology of women', in *New Introductory Lectures*, p.172.
27 Gilligan, *In a Different Voice*.
28 Schorske, *Fin de Siecle Vienna*, has a study of Klimt which includes this work, though his interpretations are very different from ours.

7 Restoring *themis* energy

1 Sherman and Strang, *Restorative Justice: The Evidence*, p.12.
2 Hesiod, *Theogony*, trs. Wender, p.30; Homer, *Iliad*, p.88; Graves, *Greek Myths*, 11, p.271, 2, pp.269–272.
3 Jung, 13: 335.
4 Jung, *Letters* 1, p.234.
5 Hesiod, *Work and Days*, trs. Wender, pp.59–60.
6 Johnstone, *A Restorative Justice Reader*, p.ix; Sherman, *Restorative Justice*; UN quoted in Johnstone, *Reader*, pp.477–478.
7 Unless specified, information on different restorative justice schemes is drawn from articles in Johnstone (ed.), *A Restorative Justice Reader*; articles in Zehr (ed.), *Critical Issues in Restorative Justice*; and Johnstone, *Restorative Justice: Ideas, Values, Debates*. Other resources: *www.restorativejustice.org* and *www.restorativejustice.org.uk* (the British Restorative Justice Consortium, includes international summaries of research on the positive effects of restorative justice on reoffending rates).
8 The story is told in Johnstone, *Ideas*, p.100.
9 Sherman, p.15, p.32.
10 Burman, 'The background of the Western legal tradition', in *Reader*, pp.108–109.
11 Ross, 'Returning to the teachings', in *Reader*, pp.125–143.
12 Yazzie and Zion, 'Navajo restorative justice', in *Reader*, pp.144–151.
13 Johnstone, *Ideas*, gives details of the different debates.
14 Hakiaha, 'What is the state's role in indigenous justice processes', in *Critical Issues*, p.355.
15 Zehr and Toews, 'Stakeholder issues' in *Critical Issues*, p.61.
16 Sherman, p.37.
17 Information on the Baltimore Community Conferencing Center is to be found at *www.communityconferencing.org*.
18 *Facing the Demons*, First Run Icarus Films.
19 Sherman, pp.26–27.
20 *Ibid.*, p.22.
21 Examples taken from Johnstone, *Ideas*, p.58.
22 Stories quoted in 'The face-to-face fix', on *www.communityconferencing.org*, and in Johnstone, *Ideas*, p.100.
23 Sherman, pp.44–45.
24 *Ibid.*, pp.88–90.

8 The road to reconciliation

1 Krog, *Country Of My Skull*, p.42, p.32. Unless specified, information on the Truth and Reconciliation Commission (TRC) comes from the seven volumes of its own reports; Boraine, *A Country Unmasked*; Krog; Rotberg and Thompson, *Truth*

v. Justice: The Morality of Truth Commissions; and Tutu, *No Future Without Forgiveness.*

2 Christie, *The South African Truth Commission*, p.1.

3 *Ibid.*, p.8.

4 Vicla-Vicenio and Verwoerd, 'Constructing the report: writing up the truth', in Rotberg and Thompson, p.281.

5 Krog, p.9.

6 Quoted in Boraine, p.362.

7 Tutu, p.35.

8 Berg, '*Ubuntu* – a contribution to the "civilisation of the universal" ', in Singer and Kimbles, p.244; Mandela, *In His Own Words*, p.324.

9 Boraine, p.258.

10 Berg, p.248.

11 *Long Night's Journey into Day: South Africa's Search for Truth & Reconciliation*, Iris Films.

12 Cynthia Ngewu, quoted in Krog, p.109.

13 Mandela, *Long Walk to Freedom*, p.751.

14 Krog, pp.110–111.

15 'Tutu bemoans failure to bring rights abusers to justice', *The Guardian*, 17.12.05, p.18.

16 de Toit, 'The moral foundations of the South African Truth and Reconciliation Commission: truth as acknowledgement and justice as recognition', in Rotberg and Thompson, pp.122–140.

17 Beth Savage, quoted in Boraine, p.8.

18 *Ibid.*

19 *Ibid.*

20 TRC, 1, p.9.

21 TRC, 5, p.352, p.353.

22 Krog, p.147.

23 Tutu, pp.116–117.

24 Krog, p.278.

25 TRC, 6, p.1.

26 Howard Jacobson, 'How exhilarating to be reminded that there is such a thing as an unpardonable crime', *The Independent*, 11.3.06, p.35.

27 The programmes, called *Facing the Truth*, were broadcast on BBC2 on 4, 5 and 6 March 2006.

28 Kiss, 'Moral ambition within and beyond political constraints', in Rotberg and Thompson, p.87.

29 Elworthy and Rifkind, *Hearts and Minds: Human Security Approaches to Political Violence*, pp.58–63.

9 Invitation to the banquet

1 Homer, *The Iliad*, p.273; Harrison, *Themis*, p.482.

2 For further thoughts on the symbolism of food, see Jackson, *Food and Transformation.*

3 See Chapter 7 for the story of Strife.

4 Aeschylus, *Prometheus Bound*, p.27; Graves, *Greek Myths* 1, p.34.

5 Graves, *ibid.*, p.144; Aeschylus, *Prometheus*, pp.28–35.

6 Ovid, *Metamorphoses*, trs. Innes, pp.35–41.

7 Genesis, 6–9; Matthew 3: 9; Luke 3: 8.

8 Hesiod, *Theogony*, trs. Wender, p.30; Kerenyi, *Gods*, p.105.

9 Ramphele, 'How does one speak of social psychology in a nation in transition?'
10 *www.theforgivenessproject.com.*
11 Pausanias, *Guide 1*, p.195.
12 Berg, 'Ubuntu', in Singer and Kimbles, p.246.
13 Appiah, *Cosmopolitanism*, p.xiii.
14 Voltaire, quoted in Appiah, p.xv.
15 Ramphele, *supra.*
16 Jung, 10: 622.
17 Appiah, p.15.
18 *www.sfcg.org.*
19 Cashford, *Hymns*, p.34.
20 Tarnas, *The Passion of the Western Mind*, p.443.
21 Cashford, *The Moon: Myth and Image*, pp.364–365.
22 Bernstein, *Living in the Borderland.*
23 Jung, *Letters 2*, p.595.

Bibliography

Editions are those cited in the text. References to Jung followed by two sets of numbers are to *The Collected Works*, eds. Herbert Reed, Michael Fordham and Gerhard Adler, trs. R.F.C. Hull, 20 vols, London: Routledge and Kegan Paul, 1959–79. The first set of numbers refers to the volume, the second to the paragraph.

Aeschylus. *Prometheus Bound*, trs. Philip Vellacott. Harmondsworth: Penguin Books, 1975.
—— *The Eumenides*, in *Oresteia*, trs. Hugh Lloyd-Jones. London: Duckworth, 1982.
Appiah, Kwame Anthony. *Cosmopolitanism: Ethics in a World of Strangers*. London: Allen Lane, 2006.
Armstrong, Karen. *A History of God*. London: Vintage, 1999.
Augustine, St. *The City of God*, 2 vols. London: Dent, 1945, 1950.
Baring, Anne and Cashford, Jules. *The Myth of the Goddess*. London: Viking Press, 1991.
Begg, Ean. *The Cult of the Black Virgin*. London: Arkana, 1985.
Berg, Astrid. '*Ubuntu* – a contribution to the "civilization of the universal" ', in Singer and Kimbles, *The Cultural Complex*.
Bernstein, Jerome, *Living in the Borderland: The Evolution of Consciousness and the Challenge of Healing Trauma*. London: Routledge, 2006.
Boraine, Alex. *A Country Unmasked: Inside the South African Truth and Reconciliation Commission*. Oxford: Oxford University Press, 2001.
Brumble, H. David. *Classical Myths and Legends in the Middle Ages and Renaissance*. London: Fitzroy Dearborn, 1998.
Burman, Harold. 'The background of the Western legal tradition', in Johnstone, *A Restorative Justice Reader*.
Campbell, Joseph. *The Hero with a Thousand Faces*. Bollingen Series XVII, 2nd edition, Princeton, NJ: Princeton University Press, 1968.
Cashford, Jules. *The Homeric Hymns*. London: Penguin Books, 2003.
Cashford, Jules. *The Moon: Myth and Image*. London: Cassell, 2003.
Christie, Kenneth. *The South African Truth Commission*. London: Macmillan, 2000.
Collins, Billy. 'Another Reason Why I Don't Keep a Gun in the House', in *The Apple That Astonished Paris*. Fayetteville: University of Arkansas Press, 1988.
Cooper, J.C. *An Encyclopaedia of Traditional Symbols*. New York: Thames and Hudson, 1979.

Curtis, Dennis E. and Resnik, Judith. 'Images of justice', in *Yale Law Journal*, PT 96, 1727–1772, 1987.

Davidson, R. J. 'Anterior electrophysiological asymmetries, emotion, and depression: conceptual and methodological conundrums', *Psychophysiology* 35, 607–614, 1998.

De Pizan, Christine. *The Book of the City of Ladies*, trs. Earl Jeffrey Richards. London: Picador /Pan Books, 1983.

Dodds, E.R. *The Greeks and the Irrational*. Berkeley: University of California Press, 1951.

Eberhard, Wolfram. *A Dictionary of Chinese Symbols*. London: Routledge, 1986.

Edinger, Edward. *The Eternal Drama: The Inner Meaning of Greek Mythology*. Boston: Shambhala, 1994.

—— *The Psyche in Antiquity, Book Two. Gnosticism and Early Christianity*. Toronto: Inner City Books, 1999.

Eliade, Mircea. (ed.) *The Encyclopaedia of Religion*. New York: Macmillan, 1987.

Elworthy, Scilla and Rifkind, Gabrielle. *Hearts and Minds: Human Security Approaches to Political Violence*. London: Demos, 2005. Available from *www.demos.co.uk*.

Encyclopaedia Judaica, Jerusalem: Encyclopaedia Judaica, 1971–2.

Euripides. *Iphigeneia in Tauris*, trs. Philip Vellacott. Harmondsworth: Penguin Books, 1972.

Ficino, Marsilio. *The Letters of Marsilio Ficino. Vol 1*. trs. by members of the School of Economic Science. London: Shepheard-Walwyn, 1975.

First Run Icarus Films. *Facing the Demons*. Brooklyn, NY, 1999.

Fontenrose, Joseph. *Python: A Study of Delphic Myth and Its Origins*. Berkley, CA: University of California Press, 1959.

—— *The Delphic Oracle: Its Responses and Operations with a Catalogue of Responses*. Berkley, CA: University of California Press, 1978.

Freud, Sigmund. 'Dreams and telepathy' in *Collected Papers IV*. London: Hogarth Press and Institute of Psychoanalysis, 1925.

—— *New Introductory Lectures on Psychoanalysis*. London: Hogarth Press and Institute of Psychoanalysis, 1933.

Geldard, Richard. *The Traveler's Key to Ancient Greece*. New York: Alfred A. Knopf, 1989, 2000.

Giegerich, Wolfgang. 'The end of meaning and the birth of man'. Guild Lecture No. 284. London: Guild of Pastoral Psychology, 2003.

Gilligan, Carol. *In a Different Voice: Psychological Theory and Women's Development*. Cambridge, MA: Harvard University Press, 1982.

Gimbutas, Marija. *The Goddesses and Gods of Old Europe: Myths and Cult Images*. London: Thames and Hudson, 1989.

Gopi Krishna. *Kundalini: The Evolutionary Energy in Man*. Boston: Shambhala, 1970.

Graves, Robert. *The Greek Myths, 2* vols. Harmondsworth: Penguin Books, 1985.

Hakiaha, Matt. 'What is the state's role in indigenous justice processes?' in Zehr and Toews, *Critical Issues in Restorative Justice*.

Handbook of the Bombay Presidency. London: John Murray, 1881.

Harrison, Jane Ellen. *Themis: A Study of the Social Origins of Greek Religion*. Cambridge: Cambridge University Press, 1927.

Heelas, Paul and Woodhead, Linda. *The Spiritual Revolution: Why Religion is Giving Way to Spirituality*. Oxford: Blackwell, 2005.

Herodotus. *The Histories*, trs. Aubrey de Selincourt. Harmondsworth: Penguin Books, 1979.

Hesiod. *Theogony and Work and Days* in *Hesiod and Theogonis*, trs. Dorothea Wender. London: Penguin Books, 1989.

Hesiod. *Theogony*, ed. M.L. West. Oxford: Clarendon Press, 1966.

Hillman, James. *The Myth of Analysis*. New York: Harper and Row, 1978.

—— 'Once more into the fray', in *Spring 56*. Connecticut: Spring Publications, 1994.

Homer. *The Iliad*, trs. E. V. Rieu. Harmondsworth: Penguin Books, 1975.

Homer. *The Odyssey*, trs. E. V. Rieu. Harmondsworth: Penguin Books, 1981.

Huskinson, Lucy. 'The self as violent other: the problem of defining the self', *Journal of Analytical Psychology* 47, 437–458, 2002.

Iris Films. *Long Night's Journey into Day: South Africa's Search for Truth and Reconciliation*. San Francisco: California Newsreel, 2000.

Jackson, Eve. *Food and Transformation: Imagery and Symbolism of Eating*. Toronto: Inner City Books, 1996.

Johnson, George. 'The feminine origins of justice and law', *Psychological Perspectives* 40, 52–69, 2000.

Johnstone, Gerry (ed). *A Restorative Justice Reader*. Cullompton, Devon: Willan, 2002.

—— *Restorative Justice: Ideas, Values, Debates*. Cullompton, Devon: Willan, 2003.

Jones, Raya. 'Jung's view of myth and post-modern psychology', *Journal of Analytical Psychology* 48, 619–628, 2003.

Jung, C.G. *Letters*, ed. Gerhard Adler. *2* vols. London: Routledge and Kegan Paul, 1973, 1975.

—— *The Visions Seminars*. 2 vols. Zurich: Spring Publications, 1976.

—— *Nietzsche's Zarathustra: Notes on the Seminar Given in 1934–1939*. Princeton: Princeton University Press, 1988.

—— *Memories, Dreams, Reflections*. London: Fontana Press, 1995.

—— *The Psychology of Kundalini Yoga*. ed. Sonu Shamdasani. London: Routledge, 1996.

Kalsched, Donald. *The Inner World of Trauma*. London: Routledge, 1996.

Kerenyi, Carl. *The Gods of the Greeks*. New York: Thames and Hudson, 1980.

Klossow de Rola, Stanislas. *Alchemy: The Secret Art*. London: Thames and Hudson, 1973.

Kramer, Heinrich and Sprenger, James. *The Malleus Maleficarum*, trs. Montague Summers. New York: Dover Publications, 1971.

Kramer, Samuel Noah. *Sumerian Mythology*. Ann Arbor: Edwards Bros., 1947.

Krog, Antjie. *Country of My Skull*. Johannesburg: Random House, 1998.

Lane, R.D., Reiman, E.M., Bradley, M.M., Lang, P.J., Ahern, G.L., Davidson, R.J., and Schwartz, G.E. 'Neuroanatomical correlates of pleasant and unpleasant emotion', *Neuropsychologia* 35, 1437–1444, 1997.

Levenson, R. and Gotman, J. 'Physiological and affective predictors of change in relationship satisfaction', *Journal of Personal and Social Psychology* 49, 85–94, 1985.

Lewis, Thomas, Armini, Fari, and Lannon, Richard. *A General Theory of Love*. New York: Vintage Books, 2000.

Lieberman, Matthew, Eisenberger, Naomi, Crockett, Molly, Tom, Sabrina, Pfeifer, Jennifer, and Way, Baldwin. 'Putting feelings into words: affect labeling disrupts amygdala activity in response to affective stimuli', *Psychological Science* 18, 421–428, 2007.

Lloyd-Jones, Hugh. *The Justice of Zeus*. Berkeley: University of California Press, 1971.

Lopez-Pedraza, Raphael. *Dionyus in Exile*. Wilmette, IL: Chiron Publications, 2000.

Lurker, Manfred. *The Gods and Symbols of Ancient Egypt*. London: Thames and Hudson, 1980.

Mandela, Nelson. *Long Walk to Freedom*. London: Abacus, 1995.

—— *In His Own Words*. London: Abacus, 2004.

McCraty, Rollin and Childre, Doc. *The Appreciative Heart: The Psychophysiology of Positive Emotions and Optimal Functioning*. HeartMath Research Center, Institute of HeartMath, Publication No. 02–026, Boulder Creek, CA, 2002.

McCraty, Rollin. *The Energetic Heart: Bioelectromagnetic Literactions Within and Between People*. HeartMath Research Center, Institute of HeartMath Publication No. 02–035, Boulder Creek, CA, 2002.

McCraty, Rollin and Tomasino, Dana. *Heart Rhythm Coherence Feedback: A New Tool for Stress Reduction, Rehabilitation, and Performance Enhancement*. Heart-Math Research Center, Institute of HeartMath, Boulder Creek, CA, 2004.

McKenna, James, Mosko, Sarah, Dungy, Claiborne, and McAninch, Jan. 'Sleep and arousal patterns of co-sleeping human mother/infant pairs: a preliminary physiological study with implications for the study of sudden infant death syndrome (SIDS)', *American Journal of Physical Anthropology* 83, 331–347, 1990.

Miller, Helen Hill. *Greek Horizons*. New York: Charles Scribner's Sons, 1961.

Mindel, Arnold. *Dreambody*. London: Routledge and Kegan Paul, 1984.

Milton, John. 'On the Morning of Christ's Nativity', in *The Poetical Works of John Milton*, ed. David Masson. London: Macmillan, 1874.

Neumann, Erich. *The Great Mother*. Bollingen Series XLVII. Princeton: Princeton University Press, 1974.

O'Neill, Onora. *Towards Justice and Virtue*. Cambridge: Cambridge University Press, 1996.

Otto, Walter. *The Homeric Gods*. London: Thames and Hudson, 1955.

Ovid. *Metamorphoses*, trs. Arthur Golding, ed. Brookes More. London: Cornhill Publishing Co., 1922.

Ovid. *Metamorphoses*, trs. Mary M. Innes. London: Penguin Books, 1955.

Parke, H.W. *A History of The Delphic Oracle*. Oxford: Blackwell, 1956.

Partin, Harry B. 'Ka'bah', in Eliade, *The Encyclopaedia of Religion*.

Pausanias. *Guide to Greece: Volumes I and 11*, trs. Peter Levi. Harmondsworth: Penguin Books, 1985.

Pendazos, Vanghelis and Sarla, Maria. *Delphi*. Athens: Yiannikos-Kaldis, 1984.

Phillips, John. *Eve: The History of an Idea*. San Francisco: Harper and Row, 1984.

Pindar. *Olympian Odes, Pythian Odes, Nemean Odes, Isthonian Odes, Fragments*. 2 vols. ed. and trs. William H. Race. Cambridge, MA: Harvard University Press, 1997.

Plato. *The Last Days of Socrates*, trs. Hugh Tredennick. London: Penguin Books, 1969.

Ramphele, Mamphela. 'How does one speak of social psychology in a nation in transition?', at XVII International Congress for Analytical Psychology IAAP, Cape Town, 13 August 2007.

Rawson, Philip. *The Art of Tantra*. London: Thames and Hudson, 1973.

Read, John. *Prelude to Chemistry*. London: G. Bell and Son, 1936.

Ripa, Caesare. *Baroque and Rococo Pictorial Imagery*, trs. Edward A. Maser. New York: Dover Publications, 1971.

Ross, Rupert. 'Returning to the teachings', in Johnstone, *A Restorative Justice Reader*.

Rossiter, Stuart. *Greece*. London: Ernest Benn, 1973.

Rotberg, Robert and Thompson, Dennis. *Truth v. Justice: The Morality of Truth Commissions*. Princeton: Princeton University Press, 2000.

Roux, Jeanne and Georges. *Greece*. Fairlawn, NJ: Essential Books, 1958.

Salman, Sherry. 'Dissociation and the self in the magical pre-Oedipal field', *Journal of Analytical Psychology* 44, 60–85, 1999.

Sanella, Lee. *The Kundalini Experience*. Lower Lake, CA: Integral Publishing, 1987.

Schorske, Carl E. *Fin de Siecle Vienna: Politics and Culture*. New York: Alfred A. Knopf, 1980.

Serrano, Miguel. *C.G. Jung and Herman Hesse: A Record of Two Friendships*. New York: Schocken, 1966.

Shamdasani, Sonu. (ed.) *C.G. Jung: The Psychology of Kundalini Yoga*. London: Routledge, 1996.

Shearer, Ann. *Athene: Image and Energy*. London: Arkana, 1998.

—— 'On the making of myths', *Journal of Jungian Theory and Practice* 6(2), 1–14, 2004.

Sheldon, Peter. *Greece*. New York: Hastings House, 1966.

Sherman, Lawrence and Strang, Heather. *Restorative Justice: The Evidence*. London: The Smith Institute, 2007.

Singer, Thomas and Kimbles, Samuel L. *The Cultural Complex*. Hove, UK: Brunner-Routledge, 2004.

Soans, Robin. *The Arab-Israeli Cookbook*. London: Aurora New Plays, 2004.

Stalley, Roger. *Early Medieval Architecture*. Oxford: Oxford University Press, 1999.

Stein, Murray. *Solar Conscience: Lunar Conscience*. Wilmette, IL: Chiron Publications, 1993.

Tarnas, Richard. *The Passion of the Western Mind*. New York: Ballentine Books, 1991.

Teicher, Martin. 'Wounds that time won't heal: the neurobiology of child abuse', in *Cerebrum* 2, 50–67, 2000.

Thomas, Keith. *Religion and the Decline of Magic: Studies in Popular Beliefs in Sixteenth- and Seventeenth-century England*. Harmondsworth: Penguin Books, 1984.

Truth and Reconciliation Commission of South Africa. *Final Report, Vols. 1–7*. Cape Town: TRC/Department of Justice, 1998–2003.

Tutu, Desmond. *No Future Without Forgiveness*. London: Rider, 1999.

Vannoy Adams, Michael. *The Mythological Unconscious*. London: Karnac, 2001.

Vicla-Vicenio, Charles and Verwoerd, Wilhelm. 'Constructing the report: writing up the truth', in Rotberg and Thompson, *Truth v. Justice: The Morality of Truth Commissions*.

Virgil, *The Eclogues*, trs. Guy Lee. London: Penguin Books, 1984.

Von Franz, Marie-Louise. *Alchemy: An Introduction to the Symbols and the Psychology*. Toronto: Inner City Books, 1980.

—— *Creation Myths*. Boston: Shambhala Publications, 1995.

Warner, Marina. *Monuments and Maidens: The Allegory of the Female Form*. London: Weidenfeld and Nicholson, 1985.

—— *From the Beast to the Blonde: On Fairy Tales and their Tellers*. London: Chatto and Windus, 1994.

Wilhelm, Richard. *I Ching or Book of Changes*. Rendered into English by Cary F. Baynes. London: Routledge and Kegan Paul, 1975.

Wood, Michael. *The Road to Delphi*. London: Chatto and Windus, 2004.

Yassie, Robert and Zion, James. 'Navajo restorative justice: the laws of equality and justice', in Johnstone, *A Restorative Justice Reader*.

Yates, Frances A. *Astraea: The Imperial Theme in the Sixteenth Century*. London: Ark Paperbacks, 1985.

Yeats, W.B. *Collected Poems*, ed. Augustine Martin. London: Vintage, 1992.

Zehr, Howard and Toews, Barb. (eds.). *Critical Issues in Restorative Justice*. Mousey, NJ: Criminal Justice Press, 2004.

Zimmer, Heinrich. *Myths and Symbols in Indian Art and Civilisation*, ed. Joseph Campbell. Princeton: Princeton University Press, 1972.

Index

Note: Page numbers in **bold** refer to figures and images.